THE CAPE COD

COOKBOOK

*210 Traditional Recipes from Chatham Cranberry Salsa
to Provincetown Crab Cakes*

JEROME RUBIN

Adams Media Corporation
Avon, Massachusetts

Published by
Adams Media, an F+W Publications Company
57 Littlefield Street, Avon, MA 02322 U.S.A.
www.adamsmedia.com

ISBN: 1-58062-584-3

Printed in Canada.

J I H G F E D C

Postcards courtesy of Jerome Rubin.

*This book is available at quantity discounts for bulk
purchases. For information, call 1-800-872-5627.*

Library of Congress Cataloging-in-Publication Data

Rubin, Jerome.
   The Cape Cod cookbook : 210 traditional recipes
from Chatham cranberry salsa to Provincetown crab
cakes / by Jerome Rubin.
     p. cm.
Includes index.
ISBN 1-58062-584-3
   1. Cookery, American. 2. Cookery—
Massachusetts. I. Title.
TX715 .R92157 2002
641.58744—dc21   2001056155

Table of Contents

Fish

Shellfish

A Bit of Cape Cod History

In 1602, an Englishman named Bartholomew Gosnold was navigating the waters off the coast of New England. One day, a tremendous school of fish swam around his ship. On the spur of the moment, he called the place they were passing *Cape Cod,* charting it so on his map. When his king heard the name, he was not pleased, and he in turn called the peninsula Cape James. But no one would call it that. Thus the name Cape Cod sticks, and so it will be called ". . . 'til shoals of codfish be seen swimming on its highest hills."

Cape Cod, the curving arm of Massachusetts, belongs as much to the ocean as it does to the continent—a kind of hinge on which the new continent swings open to the old, a little wilderness that quite unconsciously became a pivot of modern civilization. There is perhaps no annex to any other continent like it. Nowhere else is there a frail, glacial peninsula standing out 70 miles into an ocean, with bedrock so far down that no sea chiseling and no boring has ever reached a square foot of it. Upon just such a foundation were these glorious United States founded.

One of the most satisfying things about the Cape is that it is so small and the vistas so clear that it looks to the eye almost exactly as it does on the map. The climate might be called oceanic, and much is compressed into the scientific word— refreshing summers and moderately cold winters. It is a fertile land of glowing flowers and charming panoramas, but it is a land ruled by water—its sands and storms, its shrubs and trees, its people and their daily lives controlled by the sea.

The Cape Cod Canal is one of the most interesting and important features in the geography of the Cape. It is an 8-mile long waterway connecting Cape Cod Bay to the north with Buzzards Bay to the south. The canal was opened in 1914, allowing shipping to chart a shorter, safer course between Boston and New York. The canal was purchased by the federal government in 1927 and has since been maintained by the Army Corps of Engineers and patrolled by the U.S. Coast Guard.

At the opposite end of the Cape, both socially and geographically, lies Provincetown, former fishing village turned artist's colony and summer resort. The Pilgrims, who would later be known to history as the first settlers at Plymouth Plantation, landed here in 1620. In the intervening centuries, the town at the outermost point of land was a quiet fishing village, which by the beginning of the 20th century had become home to a closely knit Portuguese-American community.

Provincetown is also home to the nation's oldest continuous art colony. The colony began with Charles Hawthorne, who opened the Cape Cod School of Art in 1899. The radiant natural light and picturesque seascapes and landscapes create vistas that change with the season, offering a unique and timeless perspective for the creative soul. The original school is still thriving and attracts students and established artists from around the world.

The pages of this book portray some of the unusual and historic scenes that have made the Cape what it is and that have become a part of its legend and history. Integral to these memories are the food and recipes from this unique and special place. We hope you will enjoy these recipes and that they will enhance your memories of visiting Cape Cod.

Commercial Street, Provincetown

Appetizers and Dips

Clams Jerome

YIELD: 16 CLAMS

2 tablespoons butter

3 tablespoons olive oil

3 garlic cloves, minced

3 tablespoons minced onion

$\frac{1}{2}$ teaspoon oregano

$\frac{1}{8}$ teaspoon pepper

32 ounces chopped clams,
  with broth

2 tablespoons minced parsley

$\frac{3}{4}$ cup Italian seasoned
  breadcrumbs

3 tablespoons grated Romano
  cheese

Grated Romano cheese,
  for topping

Paprika, for topping

16 clean, well-scrubbed clam
  shells

Preheat oven to 350°F.

In 2-quart saucepan, melt butter and add olive oil. Add garlic, onion, oregano, and pepper. Simmer until onion is golden. Add clams with broth, parsley, breadcrumbs, and cheese. Simmer 5 to 10 minutes. Clam mixture should be the consistency of wet oatmeal; if too thick, add additional broth or water.

Spoon about 2 tablespoons of clam mixture into each clam shell. Top with grated cheese and paprika. Bake until brown, about 15 minutes. ᨒ

Clams à la Tonina

YIELD: 18 CLAMS

9 medium to large cherrystone clams, reserving clam juice

$1/2$ loaf Italian bread

1 egg, beaten

3 tablespoons mayonnaise

1 tablespoon chopped parsley or parsley flakes

$1/2$ teaspoon oregano

$1/2$ teaspoon garlic powder

$1/2$ teaspoon Worcestershire sauce

$1/2$ teaspoon salt

$1/2$ teaspoon black pepper

Dash liquid hot pepper sauce

1 egg, beaten, for topping

$1/4$ cup mayonnaise, for topping

Lemon wedges, for garnish

Preheat oven to 350°F.

Open clams and reserve juice. Finely chop clams. Clean both halves of shells for filling.

Remove crust from bread. Finely chop bread. Place bread in a large bowl.

In medium bowl, mix together 1 egg, 3 tablespoons mayonnaise, parsley, oregano, garlic powder, Worcestershire sauce, salt, pepper, liquid hot pepper sauce, and reserved clam juice. Add egg mixture to bread and mix well. Add chopped clams. Fill each clam shell with approximately 1 tablespoon of mixture.

Bake for about 15 minutes to heat thoroughly.

To make topping, beat egg with $1/4$ cup mayonnaise. Remove clams from oven and spread each clam with the topping. Place clams under broiler until topping is browned, about 2 to 3 minutes. Serve immediately with lemon wedges. ✑

Dill Bread

1/2 cup water

1 tablespoon sugar

1 tablespoon butter

1 1/2 teaspoons rapid-rise yeast
   (about 2/3 of 1/4-ounce packet)

1/2 cup of buttermilk

1 large egg, lightly beaten

1 1/2 teaspoons dried dill

1 teaspoon salt

3 cups bread flour

Bring water to a boil in small saucepan; remove from heat. Stir in sugar and butter. When mixture is warm (110°F to 115°F), add the yeast and mix well. Let stand until the mixture is bubbly, approximately 10 minutes.

Combine buttermilk, egg, dill, and salt in large bowl until well blended. Add yeast mixture; mix well. Add the bread flour, 1/2 cup at a time (mixing well after each addition), until dough is no longer sticky. Knead the dough until it is smooth and elastic, about 5 minutes, adding additional flour if dough is too sticky. Form the dough into a ball and place in a bowl. Cover; let rise in warm place until the ball has doubled in size, about 1 hour.

Preheat oven to 350°F and grease an 8 × 4-inch loaf pan. Punch down dough and shape into loaf. Place in prepared pan and bake until golden, about 30 to 35 minutes. Cool, then take the loaf out of the pan and put it on a rack to cool for an additional hour. ∾

Smoked Salmon Rolls

YIELD: 6 TO 12 SERVINGS

1 cup red onion, finely chopped

1 tablespoon honey

1 tablespoon white wine vinegar

4 ounces cream cheese, room temperature

3 tablespoons fresh chives, chopped

2 tablespoons sour cream

1 teaspoon dried dill

1 tablespoon capers, drained

5 flour tortillas

6 ounces smoked salmon, thinly sliced

Mix onion, honey, and vinegar together in a small bowl and set aside.

In another bowl, mix cream cheese, chives, sour cream, dill, and capers. Spread cream cheese mixture evenly on each of the 5 tortillas.

Divide salmon into 5 portions and place on each tortilla, covering half of the tortilla only. Spoon 1 tablespoon of the onion mixture over the salmon. Begin rolling the tortillas, starting with the side that is covered with salmon, until a spiral tube is formed.

Slice rolls into 1/2-inch thick slices.

Sweet Orange-Glazed Chicken Wings

YIELD: 24 APPETIZERS

12 chicken wings

1/3 cup chili sauce

1/4 cup orange marmalade

1 tablespoon red wine vinegar

1 1/2 teaspoons Worcestershire sauce

1/2 teaspoon prepared mustard

1/4 teaspoon garlic powder

Cut each chicken wing in half, and take off the wing tips. Place in plastic food storage bag. Add all remaining ingredients; seal bag. Turn bag to coat wings. Refrigerate 4 to 24 hours to marinate, turning bag occasionally.

Heat oven to 375°F. Drain chicken wings; reserve marinade. Place chicken wings on broiler pan. Bake for 45 to 60 minutes or until chicken is no longer pink, brushing occasionally with reserved marinade. Discard any remaining marinade. Serve warm. ❧

Hot Crab Dip

8 ounces regular crabmeat

8 ounces cream cheese, softened

$1/2$ cup sour cream

2 tablespoons mayonnaise

1 tablespoon lemon juice

$1^{1}/4$ teaspoons Worcestershire sauce

2 tablespoons hot sauce

$1/2$ teaspoon dry mustard

Pinch of garlic salt

Few tablespoons milk

2 tablespoons cheddar cheese, grated

Paprika, for garnish

Remove cartilage from crabmeat. In a large bowl, mix cream cheese, sour cream, mayonnaise, lemon juice, Worcestershire sauce, hot sauce, mustard, and garlic salt until smooth. Add just enough milk to make a creamy mixture. Stir in 2 tablespoons grated cheese. Fold crabmeat into cream cheese mixture. Serve with crackers. ❧

Uncle John's Crab Dip

YIELD: ABOUT 4 CUPS

1 pound cooked crabmeat

1 cup sour cream

1/2 cup mayonnaise

1/4 cup finely chopped onion

1/4 cup sweet pickle relish

1 1/2 tablespoons dark rum

Remove cartilage from crabmeat. Mix together sour cream, mayonnaise, onion, pickle relish, and rum. Add to crabmeat and mix thoroughly but gently with a fork. Chill thoroughly. Serve with crackers. ⌣

Highland Light, North Truro

Sauces, Salsas, and Jellies

À La King Sauce

YIELD: 6 TO 8 SERVINGS

1/4 cup butter

1/4 cup flour

1/2 teaspoon salt

Freshly ground pepper

2 cups milk

1 tablespoon vegetable oil

1 cup sliced mushrooms

1 cup diced green pepper

1/4 cup sherry

1/3 cup diced pimiento

1 cup cooked peas

In a medium saucepan, melt the butter. Blend in flour, salt, and pepper. Add milk. Stir over medium heat until smooth and thickened.

In a medium frying pan, heat the vegetable oil; add the mushrooms and green pepper and cook until warm. Add to the white sauce. Stir in sherry, diced pimiento, and cooked peas. Cover and cook over hot water for 10 minutes. Serve on toast points. ∾

Boston Hot

YIELD: 5 QUARTS OR 10 PINTS

1 peck ripe tomatoes, finely chopped and drained

2 cups celery, finely chopped

3 sweet red peppers, finely chopped

3 sweet green peppers, finely chopped

2 cups sweet onions, finely chopped

1 cup horseradish root

1 cup white mustard seed

1 cup brown sugar

2/3 cup salt

6 cups sugar

2 tablespoons mixed pickling spice

In a large saucepan, combine all ingredients. Heat to boiling but do not cook. Seal in sterilized jars. ⌒

Cioppino Sauce

YIELD: ABOUT 3 CUPS

3 large ripe tomatoes, chopped

1 large onion, chopped

1 green pepper, diced

1 carrot, grated

1 stalk celery, sliced

1 (8-ounce) can tomato sauce

2 tablespoons minced parsley

1 teaspoon oregano

1 crushed garlic clove

1 cup fish stock or chicken
  bouillon

1 tablespoon olive oil

1/4 cup dry red wine

Salt and pepper to taste

In a large frying pan, combine the vegetables with the tomato sauce, parsley, oregano, garlic, stock, and olive oil. Simmer, covered, for about 1 hour, stirring often. During the last 15 minutes, add the dry red wine. Season to taste with salt and pepper. If sauce becomes too thick, add a little more stock during cooking. ⌒

Cioppino Sauce (2)

4 large onions, finely chopped

2 green peppers, finely chopped

6 cloves garlic, minced

$1/4$ cup olive oil

$1/4$ pound butter

2 (16-ounce) cans stewed tomatoes, with juice

1 (8-ounce) can tomato paste

1 bottle chili sauce

2 small cans tomato sauce

1 teaspoon Worcestershire sauce

1 bay leaf

1 teaspoon chopped parsley

3 whole cloves

$1/2$ teaspoon saffron

$1/2$ teaspoon paprika

Pinch of thyme

Salt and pepper to taste

$1/2$ cup sherry

1 cup white wine

1 tablespoon grated orange rind

• • •

In a large saucepan, sauté the onions, green peppers, and garlic until tender in the olive oil and butter. Add the stewed tomatoes and juice, tomato paste, chili sauce, tomato sauce, Worcestershire sauce, bay leaf, parsley, cloves, saffron, paprika, thyme, and salt and pepper. Cook slowly for $1^{1}/_2$ hours, stirring occasionally. Add the sherry, wine, and grated orange rind and continue to cook slowly for another $1^{1}/_2$ hours.

Cocktail Sauce

YIELD: ABOUT $3/4$ CUP

$1/3$ cup chili sauce

$1/3$ cup catsup

1 teaspoon minced onion

2 teaspoons tarragon vinegar

1 tablespoon lemon juice

$1/4$ teaspoon salt

Few drops Tabasco sauce

$1/4$ to $1/2$ teaspoon sugar

1 small whole garlic clove, peeled

Combine all ingredients. Chill. Remove garlic clove before serving. ∾

Lobster fishermen, Cape Cod

Cucumber, Dill, and Caper Sauce

YIELD: ABOUT 2 CUPS

1 cup diced, seeded cucumber

2 tablespoons butter

2 tablespoons flour

2 tablespoons lemon juice

1 teaspoon grated lemon rind

1 teaspoon grated onion

$1/2$ teaspoon salt

Few grains pepper

1 tablespoon chopped fresh dill

1 tablespoon capers

In a frying pan, cook cucumber in $1/2$ cup water until tender and clear. Drain, but reserve cooking water.

In a large frying pan, melt butter; blend in flour, and add the cooking water mixture. Stir until smooth and thickened. Add remaining ingredients and the cooked cucumbers. Heat to serving temperature. ✎

Egg and Chive Sauce

YIELD: ABOUT 3 CUPS

2 cups well-seasoned medium
    white sauce (see À la king
    recipe)

1 tablespoon grated onion

3 hard cooked eggs, sliced

1 tablespoon cut chives

1 tablespoon diced pimiento

*M*ake 2 cups well-seasoned medium white sauce, adding onion to butter while melting. Add the eggs, chives, and pimiento. ～

Lemon-Butter Sauce

YIELD: ABOUT $\frac{1}{2}$ CUP

$\frac{1}{4}$ cup butter

2 tablespoons lemon juice

1 teaspoon minced onion

Dash of Tabasco sauce

Combine all ingredients and mix well. ∽

Mild Curry Sauce

YIELD: ABOUT 3 CUPS

2 cups medium white sauce
  (see À la king recipe)

1 small onion, minced

2 to 3 teaspoons of curry powder

Make 2 cups of medium white sauce, cooking the onion in the butter and adding 2 to 3 teaspoons of curry powder to the flour. ∽

Pesto Sauce

YIELD: ABOUT 1 1/2 CUPS

1 cup fresh cilantro

1 cup fresh parsley

1/2 cup pine nuts, lightly toasted

1/2 cup grated Parmesan cheese

5 cloves garlic, minced

4 jalapeño chili peppers, diced

1 teaspoon lime juice

1/2 teaspoon grated lime peel

3/4 cup olive oil

In food processor with metal blade or in blender, prepare sauce by combining cilantro, parsley, pine nuts, cheese, and garlic. Process 10 to 15 seconds to chop mixture. Add peppers, lime juice, and lime peel; process 5 to 10 seconds to blend. With machine running, add oil in a slow, steady stream through feed tube or opening in blender lid until well blended. ❧

Blueberry Chutney

YIELD: 2 CUPS

1$^1/_2$ pints (about 3 cups) fresh blueberries, sorted and washed, or frozen blueberries without sugar

$^1/_4$ cup chopped onion

1 tablespoon grated fresh gingerroot

$^1/_2$ cup firmly packed brown sugar

1 tablespoon corn starch

$^1/_3$ cup cider vinegar

$^1/_4$ teaspoon salt

1 (3-inch) cinnamon stick

In large saucepan, combine all ingredients. Bring mixture to a boil over medium heat, stirring frequently. Boil 1 minute. Remove cinnamon stick. Cool. Cover. Refrigerate. Serve as a condiment with meats and cheeses. ∾

Fish shanty, Lewis Bay, Hyannis

Cranberry Chutney

YIELD: ABOUT 2 1/2 CUPS

1 (16-ounce) can cranberry sauce
(whole berry)

1/2 cup raisins

1/2 cup peeled, diced apple

2 1/4 tablespoons sugar

2 1/4 tablespoons vinegar

1/8 teaspoon allspice

1/8 teaspoon ginger

1/8 teaspoon cinnamon

Dash cloves

Combine all ingredients in medium saucepan. Cook on medium heat, stirring occasionally, until apples are tender and sauce has thickened slightly, about 30 minutes. ∾

Cranberry Maple Chutney

YIELD: 6 TO 8 SERVINGS

$^1/_2$ cup chopped walnuts

1 cup fresh cranberries

$^3/_4$ cup water

$^1/_2$ cup maple syrup

1 Granny Smith apple,
  cored and cubed

1 fresh peach, peeled, pitted,
  and cubed

Preheat oven to 350°F. Place walnuts on a cookie sheet and toast in oven for 8 minutes, watching carefully to prevent burning.

Boil cranberries in water until soft, but not mushy, 3 to 5 minutes. Add maple syrup, apple, peach, and toasted walnuts and simmer, stirring occasionally, for 20 to 25 minutes. Serve warm or cold. ～

Chatham Cranberry Salsa

YIELD: ABOUT 2½ CUPS

1 cup water

1 cup sugar

12 ounces fresh or frozen
cranberries

2 tablespoons chopped canned
jalapeño peppers

1 teaspoon dried cilantro

¼ teaspoon ground cumin

1 green onion (scallion), green
and white parts finely sliced

1 teaspoon lime juice

Combine water and sugar in a medium saucepan. Bring to a boil over medium heat. Add cranberries; return to a boil. Gently boil cranberries for 10 minutes without stirring. Pour into a medium mixing bowl. Gently stir in remaining ingredients.

Place a piece of plastic wrap directly on salsa. Cool to room temperature and then refrigerate. Serve at room temperature. ∾

Minty Cranberry Relish

2 large apples

1 (12-ounce) package fresh
   cranberries

1 cup packed fresh mint

1/2 cup firmly packed light
   brown sugar

2/3 cup orange marmalade

2 tablespoons lemon juice

2 tablespoons Dijon mustard

1 cup golden raisins

Peel and core apple. Cut in 16 pieces.
Combine apple pieces, cranberries, and mint in bowl or food processor; process using on/off pulsing action until chopped into medium-sized chunks. Transfer cranberry-apple mixture to medium bowl. Combine brown sugar, orange marmalade, lemon juice, and Dijon mustard in medium bowl. Stir until well blended, add marmalade mixture to cranberry-apple mixture, and stir until well blended. Add raisins and stir well.

Store relish in tightly covered container in refrigerator. Serve relish well chilled. ∾

Esther's Plum Jelly

YIELD: 12 JELLY GLASSES

5 pounds ripe tart plums,
  washed and pitted

1$\frac{1}{2}$ cups water

1 box pectin

7$\frac{1}{2}$ cups sugar

Place plums in kettle. Add water, cover, and simmer for 10 minutes. Pour cooked plums into food processor and crush. Strain 5$\frac{1}{2}$ cups juice through 3 layers of cheesecloth 2 times until jelly is extremely clear. Mix pectin with juice in saucepan. Over high heat, bring mixture to a hard boil, stirring occasionally. Immediately add sugar. Bring to full rolling boil and boil hard 1 minute, stirring constantly.

Remove from heat. Set aside for 10 minutes. Skim off foam with metal spoon. Pour at once into sterilized glasses and seal. ∾

Shrimp Vinaigrette

YIELD: 6 SERVINGS

1 pound large shrimp with shells

6 cloves garlic, minced

1/3 cup lemon juice

1/3 cup olive oil

1 tablespoon minced fresh Italian parsley

1 1/2 teaspoons minced fresh thyme

1 1/2 teaspoons grated lemon peel

Kosher (coarse) salt and freshly ground black pepper

Bring a large pot to a boil. Add shrimp and cook just until bright orange, about 2 minutes. Drain and set aside. In bowl, whisk garlic with lemon juice, oil, parsley, thyme, and lemon peel. Season to taste with salt and pepper. Add shrimp and toss to coat. Refrigerate several hours, tossing occasionally.

Beatrice House, Oak Bluffs

Salads

Blue Cheese Potato Salad

YIELD: THIRTEEN $1/2$-CUP SERVINGS

5 cups quartered, cooked small
  red potatoes

4 ounces (1 cup) crumbled blue
  cheese

$3/4$ cup reduced-calorie
  mayonnaise

$1/2$ cup light dairy sour cream

2 tablespoons chopped fresh
  chervil or parsley

$1/4$ teaspoon salt (optional)

1 tablespoon cider vinegar

1 tablespoon Dijon mustard

$3/4$ cup sliced radishes

Lettuce, for garnish (optional)

In large bowl, combine potatoes and blue cheese; toss gently. In small bowl, combine mayonnaise, sour cream, chervil, salt, vinegar, and mustard and blend well. Add to potato mixture and mix well. Cover and refrigerate 1 hour to blend flavors. Stir in radishes just before serving. Serve in lettuce-lined bowl, if desired. ∾

Chicken Gazpacho Salad

YIELD: 4 SERVINGS

3 tablespoons lemon juice

3 tablespoons olive oil

1 1/2 teaspoons chopped fresh basil, or 1/2 teaspoon dried basil

1/4 teaspoon salt

3 to 4 drops hot pepper sauce

1 clove garlic, minced

3 green onions, sliced

2 medium tomatoes, seeded, chopped

1 small cucumber, halved lengthwise, thinly sliced

1 medium green pepper, chopped

4 boneless chicken breast halves (about 1 pound)

4 cups torn salad greens

In medium bowl, combine all ingredients except chicken and salad greens; mix well. Set aside.

Heat broiler. Place 1 chicken breast half between 2 pieces of plastic wrap or waxed paper. Working from center, gently pound chicken with flat side of meat mallet or rolling pin until about 1/4 inch thick; remove wrap. Repeat with remaining chicken breast halves.

When ready to broil, place chicken breast halves on broiler pan 4 to 6 inches from heat for 6 to 10 minutes or until chicken is no longer pink and juices run clear, turning once.

When ready to serve, arrange salad greens on 4 plates. Stir vegetable mixture. Using slotted spoon, arrange vegetable mixture over greens. Arrange chicken slices over vegetable mixture. Spoon liquid from vegetable mixture over chicken. ❧

Chilled Vegetable Salad

YIELD: 8 SERVINGS

Dressing:

2 cloves garlic

1/4 cup freshly squeezed lemon
juice

1 tablespoon chopped fresh
oregano

1 tablespoon tomato paste

1/2 teaspoon chopped fresh
rosemary

1/8 teaspoon black pepper

1 cup olive oil

Salad:

1/2 head of cauliflower, cut into
florets

1 cup sliced cooked green beans

1 cup cooked sliced carrots

1/2 cup sliced green pepper

3/4 cup thinly sliced celery

2 large green onions, thinly sliced

1/2 cup sliced mushrooms

1/2 cup pitted black olives, drained

1/2 cup sliced pimientos

• • •

To prepare the dressing, peel and mince garlic. In a shallow glass bowl, combine all dressing ingredients except olive oil. Mix well. Whisk in olive oil until well blended.

Combine all salad ingredients in extra-large mixing bowl. Toss gently. Pour dressing over salad and toss well to coat all vegetables. Cover and refrigerate overnight. Serve chilled. ✑

Citrus Poppy Seed Vinaigrette Salad

YIELD: 10 SERVINGS

Vinaigrette:

1/4 cup orange juice

2 tablespoons white wine
    vinegar

2 green onions, chopped

1/3 cup sugar

1/4 teaspoon salt

1/3 cup oil

1 tablespoon poppy seeds

Salad:

8 cups torn romaine lettuce
    leaves

1 cup cubed honeydew melon

1 cup cubed cantaloupe

1 cup halved strawberries

In blender or food processor fitted with metal blade, combine orange juice, vinegar, onions, sugar, and salt; cover and blend well. With machine running, slowly drizzle in oil, blending until smooth. Add poppy seeds; blend for a few seconds until thoroughly mixed.

In a large serving or salad bowl, combine all salad ingredients; toss to mix. Pour dressing over salad; toss to coat.

Crab and Papaya Salad

YIELD: 8 SERVINGS

4 ripe papayas

2 lemons

16 large leaves leaf lettuce, for garnish

2 pounds cooked crabmeat

Seafood Dressing (see next recipe)

16 carrot curls, for garnish

Parsley sprigs, for garnish

Halve the papayas crosswise and remove seeds. Cut $1/4$ inch from bottom of each half so papayas will sit and not roll. Quarter the lemons and squeeze $1/4$ of a lemon over each papaya half to prevent discoloring and add flavor. Wash the lettuce leaves, dry, and line 8 individual serving plates.

Remove cartilage from crabmeat. In large bowl, combine crabmeat with 1 cup of Seafood Dressing, mixing thoroughly but gently. Divide crabmeat mixture evenly among papaya halves, filling cavities with the mixture. Place each papaya half in center of individual serving plate; garnish with carrot curls. Spoon 1 tablespoon of Seafood Dressing over crabmeat and garnish with parsley sprigs. Serve remaining Seafood Dressing on the side. ◞

Megathlin's Drugstore, Main Street, Hyannis

Seafood Dressing

YIELD: ABOUT 3 1/2 CUPS

2 (8-ounce) packages cream
cheese

1 cup mayonnaise

1/4 cup sour cream

1/3 cup chopped pimiento

1 clove garlic, minced

1 tablespoon chopped onion

1 tablespoon soy sauce

1/2 tablespoon bitters

1/2 tablespoon liquid hot pepper
sauce

1/4 teaspoon chicken stock

In large bowl soften cream cheese. Add mayonnaise and sour cream and mix until mixture is smooth. Add remaining ingredients and blend well. Chill for at least 12 hours before using. ✎

Green Bean Hazelnut Salad

1/3 cup oil

1/4 cup cider vinegar

2 teaspoons sugar

1/4 teaspoon salt

1/4 teaspoon dried basil

1 teaspoon Dijon mustard

1 pound (16 ounces) fresh or
   frozen green beans, cooked
   and drained

2 cups cherry tomatoes, halved

1 cup hazelnuts (filberts), toasted

In large bowl, combine oil, vinegar, sugar, salt, basil, and mustard; blend well. Add cooked beans; toss well to coat. Cover and refrigerate overnight. Just before serving, stir in tomatoes and hazelnuts. ～

Hot Scallop and Spinach Salad

YIELD: 4 SERVINGS

6 to 7 ounces fresh spinach
leaves

4 ounces blue cheese,
Gorgonzola, or feta cheese,
crumbled

1 pound scallops

2 teaspoons olive oil

1/2 cup Italian salad dressing

1/3 cup walnuts, coarsely
chopped

Thoroughly rinse and pat dry spinach leaves. Remove stems. Divide the leaves among 4 large salad plates. Sprinkle crumbled cheese over leaves.

Rinse scallops and pat dry. Slice large scallops in half, horizontally. Heat olive oil in large frying pan over high heat. When hot, add half of the scallops and cook, stirring often, until opaque through center (cut to test), 1 to 2 minutes. Lift scallops from pan and set aside. Repeat with remaining scallops, adding more oil if needed. Bring dressing to a simmer over medium heat. Arrange scallops on spinach, drizzle with hot dressing, and sprinkle with nuts. ∾

Lentil Salad

YIELD: SEVEN 1-CUP SERVINGS

Dressing:

1/3 cup olive oil

1/3 cup balsamic or cider vinegar

1/2 teaspoon salt

1/8 teaspoon coarsely ground
   black pepper

2 dashes hot pepper sauce

2 cloves garlic, minced

Salad:

1 cup uncooked lentils

2 cups water

1 (7-ounce) package uncooked
   tortellini

1/2 cup chopped fresh parsley

1/2 cup thinly sliced green onions

2 tablespoons chopped fresh oregano, or 2 teaspoons
   dried oregano

1 medium tomato, chopped and seeded

• • •

In jar with tight-fitting lid, combine all dressing ingredients; shake well.

Sort and rinse lentils. In 2-quart saucepan, bring water to a boil; stir in lentils. Reduce heat. Cover and simmer for 15 to 20 minutes, or until lentils are tender but not mushy. Drain.

Meanwhile, cook tortellini according to directions on package. Drain. Rinse with cold water. In large bowl, combine all salad ingredients and toss. Pour dressing over salad; toss to coat. Cover. Refrigerate 3 hours or until chilled. If desired, garnish with additional parsley and oregano.

Harvesting cranberries, Cape Cod

My Grandma's Coleslaw

YIELD: 6 SERVINGS

Salad:

3 cups shredded cabbage

$1/3$ cup chopped celery

$1/3$ cup chopped green pepper

2 tablespoons chopped pimiento

Dressing:

$1/4$ cup sugar

2 tablespoons water

$1/4$ teaspoon celery seed

$1/8$ teaspoon salt

$1/8$ teaspoon mustard seed

In small saucepan, bring dressing ingredients to a boil. Remove from heat; cool. In a large bowl, combine salad ingredients and mix well. Pour cooled dressing over salad and toss well to coat. Refrigerate several hours to blend flavors. ❧

Red Potato Salad

YIELD: 8 TO 12 SERVINGS

3 pounds red baby potatoes

1 cup chopped shallots

2 tablespoons snipped fresh dill

$1/2$ cup chopped fresh basil

1 tablespoon Italian herb blend (spices)

$2/3$ cup olive oil

$1/2$ cup balsamic vinegar

Salt and pepper to taste

Scrub and quarter the potatoes. Poach potatoes in lightly salted, gently boiling water until tender but not soft, 25 to 30 minutes. Drain potatoes and rinse in cold running water to stop cooking.

Toss potatoes with shallots in a large mixing bowl. In a separate bowl, mix herbs, oil, and vinegar. Add salt and pepper to taste. Pour over potatoes and shallots and toss well to combine. Cover and refrigerate overnight. ᴖ

Salmon and Asparagus Pasta Salad

YIELD: 4 SERVINGS

Salad:

5 ounces (2 cups) uncooked
rotini (spiral pasta)

$1/2$ pound fresh asparagus,
trimmed, cut into $1^{1}/_{2}$-inch
pieces

2 medium Italian plum
tomatoes, coarsely chopped

8 ounces of cooked, boned
salmon or canned salmon with
skin and bones removed

2 tablespoons sliced green
onions

Leaf lettuce

Dressing:

$1/3$ cup mayonnaise

2 tablespoons milk

1 tablespoon honey mustard

1 tablespoon white wine

$1/2$ teaspoon dried dill weed

• • •

In a large saucepan, cook pasta as directed on package, adding asparagus during last 3 to 5 minutes of cooking time. Cook until rotini pasta and asparagus are tender. Drain; rinse with cold water to cool. Drain well.

In large bowl, combine cooked pasta and asparagus, tomatoes, salmon, and onions. Mix well.

In small bowl, combine all dressing ingredients; blend well with wire whisk. Pour dressing over salad, tossing gently to coat. If desired, season with salt and pepper. Cover and refrigerate for at least 30 minutes to blend flavors. To serve, arrange lettuce on individual salad plates and top with portions of salad. ∾

Seafood Rice Salad

YIELD: 6 SERVINGS

4 cups chicken broth

2 garlic heads, halved crosswise

2 cups rice

1/2 cup squid, cut into rings

1/2 pound medium shrimp, shelled and deveined

1/2 pound bay scallops

8 mussels, scrubbed

8 clams, scrubbed

1 medium tomato, seeded and diced

1/2 cup diced celery

1/2 cup sliced green onion

Juice and grated peel of 1 lemon

1/2 cup olive oil

Kosher (coarse) salt and freshly ground black pepper

1/2 cup julienned fresh basil leaves

In large saucepan, bring broth to a boil with 2 garlic halves. Add the rice and return to a boil. Stir, reduce heat, cover, and simmer about 20 minutes or until rice is cooked through. Remove garlic and set aside. Spread rice on baking sheet and allow to cool.

Bring a medium-large pot of water to a boil with one of the 2 remaining garlic halves. Drop squid into water and cook just until opaque, less than 1 minute. Remove with slotted spoon and cool. Add shrimp to water and cook just until bright orange. Remove and cool. Drop in scallops and cook just until opaque. Remove and cool.

(continued)

. . . continued

In large skillet, bring about ³/₄-inch water to boil with remaining garlic half. Add mussels and clams; cover, and steam just until shells open. Remove and cool. Remove shells, if desired. In large bowl, combine cooled rice and seafood; add tomato, celery, and green onion.

In blender, combine lemon juice and peel with olive oil. Squeeze cloves from garlic reserved from cooking rice and add to blender. Process until blended. Season to taste with salt and pepper. Add to rice mixture along with basil. Toss to combine thoroughly. Serve at room temperature or chill up to several hours and serve cold. ☙

Shrimp and Fruit Celebration Salad

YIELD: TWELVE 1-CUP SERVINGS

Salad:

6 ounces (2 cups) uncooked shell
macaroni

12 ounces medium cooked
shrimp

1 1/2 cups chopped celery

1/2 cup chopped green pepper

Leaf lettuce

3 large peaches or nectarines

Dressing:

1/2 cup oil

1/3 cup cider vinegar

1 teaspoon prepared mustard

1 teaspoon salt

1 (4-ounce) jar sliced pimientos,
drained

1 clove garlic, minced

To prepare salad, cook macaroni to desired doneness, as directed on package. Drain; rinse with cold water. In large bowl, combine all salad ingredients, except lettuce and peaches; toss to combine.

In jar with tight-fitting lid, combine all dressing ingredients; shake well. Pour dressing over salad; toss to combine. Cover and refrigerate at least 1 hour to blend flavors. To serve, arrange lettuce leaves in a large salad bowl or on a platter. Mound salad over lettuce leaves. Arrange fruit slices around edge of salad.

Tricolor Summertime Pasta Salad

16 ounces tricolor pasta twists

1 each small (or $1/2$ large) green bell pepper and red bell pepper

1 small red onion, sliced thin

1 cup sliced black olives

4 to 8 ounces cheddar cheese, cubed

$1/2$ cup olive oil

$1/2$ cup red wine vinegar

1 teaspoon dried basil

1 teaspoon dried oregano

2 to 3 garlic cloves, minced

$1/2$ teaspoon dried mustard

Prepare pasta according to directions on package. Rinse with cold water and drain well. Prepare vegetables and cheese and set aside in a large bowl. In a small bowl, combine the oil, vinegar, basil, oregano, garlic, and mustard. Mix well. Add the pasta to the vegetables in the large bowl and pour on the dressing. Toss thoroughly. Refrigerate, covered, for 2 hours or overnight before serving. ∾

Orleans Harbor

Soups and Stews

Autumn Bisque

YIELD: 6 SERVINGS

1 pound butternut squash, peeled, halved, seeded, and cubed

2 tart apples

1 medium onion, chopped

2 slices white bread, crusts removed and cubed

4 cups chicken broth

$1/2$ teaspoon salt

$1/4$ teaspoon pepper

$1/4$ teaspoon dried rosemary, crushed

$1/4$ teaspoon dried marjoram, crushed

2 egg yolks, slightly beaten

$1/4$ cup heavy whipping cream

Thin apple slices (optional)

Fresh rosemary (optional)

In a large saucepan, combine the squash, apples, onion, bread cubes, chicken broth, salt, pepper, rosemary, and marjoram. Bring to a boil. Reduce heat and simmer, uncovered, for about 35 minutes, or until squash and apples are tender. Remove from heat; cool slightly.

Spoon $1/3$ of the soup into a blender or food processor. Cover and purée. Repeat with the remaining soup. Return all the puréed mixture to the saucepan and reheat gently over low heat.

In a small bowl, stir together the egg yolks and whipping cream. Beat in 1 cup of the hot soup. Then add the yolk mixture to the saucepan, stirring constantly. Heat until hot. Do not allow the soup to boil. Serve immediately. ⌒

Buzzards Bay Bouillabaisse

1 pound fresh pollock fillets

1 pound fresh cod fillets

1 pound fresh ocean perch fillets

3/4 cup chopped onion

3/4 cup sliced celery

1 large garlic clove, minced

1/3 cup butter

6 cups clam broth

3 cups fish stock

2 (16-ounce) cans peeled
  tomatoes

1/2 teaspoon dried thyme

1 large bay leaf, crushed

1/2 teaspoon saffron

1 pound fresh sea scallops

Salt and pepper to taste

2 small lobsters

Cut fillets into 2-inch pieces. In a Dutch oven, cook onion, celery, and garlic in butter until soft but not brown. Add clam broth, fish stock, tomatoes, herbs, and fish. Bring to a boil. Reduce heat and simmer 10 minutes. Add scallops and simmer 10 minutes longer. Season to taste with salt and pepper. Meanwhile, boil lobsters separately. Crack claws. Remove meat from tails and chop. Add lobster meat to soup just before serving.

Cape Cod Bouillabaisse

YIELD: 6 SERVINGS

2 large garlic cloves, crushed

$1/2$ cup chopped celery

$1/2$ cup chopped onion

$1/2$ cup chopped green pepper

$1/4$ cup olive oil

2 bay leaves

$1/2$ tablespoon oregano

$1/4$ cup fresh parsley

$1/2$ teaspoon crushed red pepper

1 teaspoon salt

1 (24-ounce) can chopped tomatoes

4 ounces clam juice

2 cups water

$1/2$ cup sherry

$1/2$ pound medium shrimp

1 pint standard oysters, shucked

$1/2$ pound white fish fillets, cut into chunks

$1/2$ pound crabmeat

6 littleneck clams, scrubbed

6 mussels, scrubbed

$1/2$ pound squid, cut into 1-inch squares

• • •

In a large 4-quart pot, sauté garlic, celery, onion, and green pepper in oil until tender. Add bay leaves, oregano, parsley, pepper, salt, and tomatoes. Simmer for 1 hour. Add clam juice, water, and sherry and simmer for 10 minutes. Add shrimp, oysters, and fish and simmer for 3 minutes. Add crabmeat, clams, mussels, and squid. Simmer until clams and mussels open. Serve immediately. ∽

Cape Cod's Jambalaya

YIELD: 4 SERVINGS

1 cup eggplant, cut in $1/2$-inch cubes

1 cup chopped orange peppers

1 medium onion, chopped

1 clove garlic, crushed

2 tablespoons olive oil

2 cups peeled, crushed tomatoes

4 cups water

$1/2$ cup long grain rice

Bay leaf

1 teaspoon dried basil

$1/2$ teaspoon chili powder

Hot pepper sauce to taste

1 pound fresh shrimp, cleaned and deveined

$1/2$ pound scallops

1 pound lobster meat

1 pound fresh codfish, skinned and boned, cut into large chunks

In a Dutch oven or stockpot, sauté the eggplant, peppers, onion, and garlic in olive oil over low to medium heat for 5 to 6 minutes, stirring often. Add tomatoes, water, rice, herbs, and seasonings. Bring to a boil; reduce heat, and simmer over low heat for 30 minutes. Add remaining ingredients and simmer an additional 5 to 8 minutes, or just until fish is opaque, but tender. Let stand 20 minutes before serving. ∾

Cape's Own Jambalaya

YIELD: 6 SERVINGS

3/4 cup chopped green pepper

1/4 cup chopped celery

1/2 cup chopped onion

3 tablespoons butter

1/2 cup fresh chopped parsley

3 tomatoes, chopped

2 cups water

1 1/2 teaspoons chicken stock

1/2 teaspoon salt

1/2 teaspoon pepper

1/2 teaspoon chili powder

2 bay leaves

2 cups cooked rice

1 pint oysters, drained

1/2 pound white fish, cut into chunks

1 pound crabmeat, cartilage removed

Sauté green pepper, celery, and onion in butter for 5 minutes in a large saucepan. Add parsley, tomatoes, water, broth, and seasonings and simmer over medium heat for 30 to 40 minutes. Add rice, oysters, and fish and simmer for 10 minutes. Add crabmeat and simmer for 5 minutes.

Carrot Ginger Soup

YIELD: 8 SERVINGS

2 tablespoons olive oil

1 cup coarsely chopped onion

1 tablespoon peeled, minced
   fresh gingerroot

1/4 cup long grain rice

1 teaspoon curry powder

2 pounds carrots, peeled and
   sliced 1/4 inch thick

10 cups defatted chicken broth

1/4 cup heavy cream

Salt and freshly ground black
   pepper to taste

Fresh mint, for garnish

Heat the oil in a stockpot. Add onion and ginger and cook for 10 minutes, stirring. Add the rice and curry powder. Cook for 1 minute, stirring constantly. Add carrots and broth. Bring to a boil; reduce heat, and simmer until carrots are tender, about 30 minutes. Remove from heat and cool.

Puree the soup in batches in a blender or food processor. Return to stockpot. Add cream and season to taste with salt and pepper. Reheat but do not boil prior to serving. Garnish individual servings with a sprig of mint.

Chunky Potato Soup

YIELD: 8 SERVINGS

3 medium red potatoes

2 cups water

1 small onion

3 tablespoons butter

3 tablespoons all-purpose flour

Crushed red pepper flakes

Ground black pepper

3 cups milk

1/2 teaspoon sugar

1 cup sharp cheddar cheese, shredded

1 cup cube cooked ham

Peel potatoes and cut into 1-inch cubes. Bring water to a boil in large saucepan. Add potatoes and cook until tender. Drain reserving liquid into container for later; set aside.

Peel and finely chop onion. Melt butter in saucepan over medium heat. Add onion to saucepan and cook, stirring frequently, until onion is translucent and tender but not brown. Add flour to saucepan. Season with pepper flakes and black pepper to taste. Cook 3 to 4 minutes.

Gradually add potatoes, reserved 1 cup cooking liquid, milk, and sugar to onion mixture in saucepan; still well. Add cheese and ham, and simmer over low heat for 30 minutes, stirring frequently. Store leftovers, covered, in refrigerator. ∾

Cold Fruit Soup

YIELD: 6 SERVINGS

1 pound fresh ripe peaches,
   washed, halved, and pitted

1 pound fresh ripe plums,
   washed, halved, and pitted

1 quart water

1 quart red wine

1 pound sugar

2-inch cinnamon stick

2 teaspoons powdered arrowroot

1 cup heavy cream

Place the fruit in a stainless steel stockpot and cover with water and wine. Add sugar and cinnamon. Cook until fruit is soft. Remove from heat and cool until workable. Work fruit through sieve, removing skins and reserving all liquid. Reheat fruit pulp and liquid. Mix a little of the cold fruit mixture with the arrowroot and stir into rest of juice. Bring to a boil, reduce heat, and simmer, stirring, for 2 minutes.

Remove from heat and cool. Refrigerate until thoroughly chilled before serving. Serve in large soup plates garnished with unsweetened whipped cream. ∾

Corn and Cheddar Chowder

YIELD: 6 SERVINGS

1 medium onion

1 medium red bell pepper

1 tablespoon butter

2 tablespoons all-purpose flour

2$1/2$ cups chicken broth

1 (16-ounce) can creamed corn

1 cup whole kernel corn

$1/2$ teaspoon hot pepper sauce

$3/4$ cup shredded sharp cheddar
cheese

Freshly ground black pepper to
taste

Chop onion and set aside. Chop the red bell pepper and place in a small bowl. Cover and refrigerate until ready to use.

Melt the butter in large saucepan over medium heat. Add onion; cook and stir about 5 minutes; sprinkle onion with flour. Cook and stir 1 minute. Add chicken broth to saucepan. Bring mixture to a boil, stirring frequently. Add creamed corn, corn kernels, red bell pepper, and hot sauce; reduce heat to low. Cover and simmer chowder an additional 15 minutes and remove saucepan from heat.

Gradually stir in cheddar until melted; ladle into soup bowls. Sprinkle with black pepper to taste. ∾

Fishing shacks, Cape Cod

Corn and Pumpkin Soup

YIELD: 10 SERVINGS

8 cups chicken broth

3 packages frozen corn niblets

1/4 cup finely chopped onion

2 tablespoons finely chopped
 jalapeño peppers

1 (16-ounce) can pumpkin

1 cup half-and-half

1/2 teaspoon salt

1/4 teaspoon pepper

10 (6 or 8-inch) corn tortillas or
 8-inch flour tortillas, warmed

In large saucepan, prepare the soup by combining broth, corn, onion, and peppers; bring to a boil. Reduce heat; cover, and simmer 20 to 25 minutes, or until onions and pepper are tender. Stir in pumpkin, blending well. Cover and simmer 5 to 10 minutes or until thoroughly heated. Add half-and-half, salt, and pepper. Heat just until hot, making sure not to boil.

To serve, line 10 soup bowls with warmed tortillas and ladle hot soup into tortilla-lined bowls. Spoon scant 2 tablespoons pesto sauce (see page 19) onto each serving. ∾

Cream of Crawfish Soup

1/2 cup finely chopped onion

1/4 cup melted butter

1/2 cup flour

2 cups chicken stock

4 cups light cream

1 pound crawfish tails, finely ground

1/2 bunch green onions, chopped

1 1/4 teaspoons onion powder

1 1/4 teaspoons garlic powder

1/8 teaspoon cayenne pepper

In a skillet, sauté onion in butter for 3 to 5 minutes. Add flour and cook 5 minutes over medium heat. Add chicken stock and cook 5 minutes. Slowly whisk in cream, stirring constantly. Season crawfish tails with the green onions, onion powder, garlic powder, and cayenne pepper. Add seasoned crawfish tails to skillet and cook over low heat, stirring constantly, for 15 minutes or until just thoroughly heated. Do not boil. ∽

Creamy Acorn Squash Soup

YIELD: 6 SERVINGS

3 tablespoons olive oil

1 shallot, minced

2 1/2 pounds acorn squash,
   peeled, seeded, and diced

3 bay leaves

1 teaspoon ground nutmeg

6 cups chicken broth

Grated zest from 1 medium
   orange

1 cup whipping cream

Fresh rosemary, for garnish

Heat oil in a large, heavy saucepan over medium heat. Add shallot and sauté until tender. Add squash and cook for 5 minutes, stirring frequently. Stir in bay leaves, nutmeg, and chicken broth. Bring to a boil. Reduce heat and simmer for 25 to 30 minutes, or until squash is soft. Remove bay leaves and let cool slightly.

Add orange zest to squash mixture. Puree soup, in batches, in blender or food processor. Return soup to saucepan and whisk in cream. Stir frequently over medium-low heat until hot. Do not boil. Garnish individual servings with a sprig of fresh rosemary.

Erwtensoep (Pea Soup)

YIELD: 6 TO 8 SERVINGS

1 pound quick-cooking green
split peas

3 quarts water

1½ tablespoons salt

½ teaspoon black pepper

¼ teaspoon allspice

¼ teaspoon marjoram

3 leeks, halved lengthwise, and
then sliced 1-inch thick

1 medium onion, thinly sliced

1 cup celery, chopped

2 pounds spareribs, cut into 2-rib
pieces

1 pound smoked sausage links

Croutons

Chopped parsley

In a 6-quart stockpot, bring peas and water to a boil. Reduce heat and simmer, covered, for 1¼ hours. Add seasonings, leeks, onion, and celery. Trim excess fat from spareribs and add to soup with sausages. Simmer 30 minutes, covered, until spareribs are tender.

To serve as a main dish soup, remove meat from spareribs, peel sausages, and slice thinly. Return to soup and serve with croutons.

To serve as two courses, remove spareribs and sausages from soup. Serve soup in bowls sprinkled with parsley and croutons. Then serve spareribs and sausages, cut into 2-inch pieces, as a main course along with potatoes and a vegetable.

Four Onion Potato Soup

YIELD: 8 SERVINGS

1/2 cup unsalted butter

2 medium onions, thinly sliced

2 cups sliced leeks

1/2 cup minced shallots

1 pound red potatoes

6 cups chicken stock

1 cup heavy cream

1 cup light cream

1/2 cup sliced scallions, plus
  greens

Salt and pepper to taste

In a large pot, melt the butter over medium heat. Add onions, leeks, and shallots and cook until onions are golden, stirring often. Meanwhile, quarter the potatoes and add these to the soup pot with enough chicken stock to cover the potatoes and onions. Heat the soup to a boil over medium heat. Reduce heat to a simmer and cook for 15 minutes, or until potatoes are just tender. Remove 3 cups of the soup with some vegetables, puree in a food processor, and return to the soup pot.

To serve chilled, remove from heat and cool the soup base completely. Refrigerate until chilled. Stir in light and heavy cream and scallions, and season with salt and pepper. Serve cold.

To serve hot, add the light and heavy cream and scallions, and season with salt and pepper. Cook gently until heated through and serve hot. ❧

Lobster Bisque

YIELD: 3 SERVINGS

1^{1}/2 cups chicken stock

1/2 cup chopped carrots

1/2 cup chopped potatoes

1/2 cup chopped onions

Pinch of white pepper

1/4 teaspoon Italian seasoning

Salt to taste

3 tablespoons white wine

1/2 cup cream

1/2 cup milk

1/2 pound lobster meat,
uncooked and chopped

Bring chicken stock to a simmer. Add chopped vegetables and simmer until tender. Pour contents of pan into blender and puree. Transfer back to saucepan and add seasonings, wine, cream, and milk. Add lobster and cook over low heat for 20 minutes. Serve hot.

Cranberry picking, Cape Cod

Lobster Bisque Atlantic

YIELD: 4 SERVINGS

2 tablespoons butter

1 medium onion, sliced

1 leek, chopped

1 carrot, sliced

1 stalk celery, chopped

$1/2$ teaspoon thyme

1 bay leaf

1 teaspoon salt

2 cups white wine

$1/2$ cup cognac

1 cup cooked rice

$1/2$ cup light cream

2 egg yolks, beaten

Meat from 2 small boiled lobsters

Melt butter in 2-quart saucepan. Add onion, leek, carrot, and celery and cook over medium heat for 3 minutes, stirring to prevent browning. Add herbs and seasoning, and continue stirring over low heat for 5 minutes. Add white wine and $1/4$ cup cognac and simmer, stirring occasionally, for 15 minutes. Remove from heat. Cool. Remove bay leaf. Puree in a food processor and return to soup pot. Add rice and cream and heat, stirring. Add remaining cognac and egg yolks. Do not boil. Add chopped lobster meat and heat thoroughly. Remove from heat and serve immediately.

Narragansett Seafood Gumbo

YIELD: 6 SERVINGS

3 tablespoons butter

3 tablespoons flour

6 cups water

1 (10-ounce) package okra,
   thawed and chopped

2 cups chopped onion

3/4 cup sliced carrots

3/4 cup chopped celery

3 tomatoes, chopped

1 clove garlic, minced

2 tablespoons chicken stock

3 bacon strips, fried and
   crumbled

1 tablespoon lemon juice

1/2 teaspoon seafood seasoning

1/2 teaspoon oregano

1/4 teaspoon ground thyme

Salt and pepper to taste

1/2 pound medium shrimp, peeled

1 pint oysters with liquor

1 pound crabmeat, cartilage removed

• • •

In a small heavy pan, prepare roux by melting butter and gradually blending in flour. Cook over medium heat until mixture turns a golden brown (about 5 minutes), stirring often.

In a large stew pot, heat water to boiling. Add vegetables, garlic, chicken stock, bacon, lemon juice, seasonings, and roux. Reduce heat to medium-low and simmer for about 45 minutes, uncovered, stirring occasionally. Add shrimp and oysters and simmer for 5 minutes. Add crabmeat and simmer for 5 minutes. Serve immediately. Serve with rice if desired.

New Bedford Chowder

YIELD: 6 SERVINGS

1/4 cup butter

1/2 cup chopped onion

1 cup chopped peeled tomatoes

1/2 cup chopped green pepper

1 bay leaf, crumbled

1/4 cup chopped parsley

1/4 teaspoon grated nutmeg

1/2 to 1 lemon, sliced

1 pound sea scallops, sliced

3 cups chicken broth

12 ounces shucked oysters, liquid reserved

1 to 2 tablespoons flour (optional)

Melt butter. Add onion and cook gently until softened. Add tomatoes, green pepper, bay leaf, parsley, and nutmeg. Cook, stirring, until hot and softened. Add lemon slices to taste. (The full lemon creates a deliciously tart flavor, but less may be used.) Then add scallops and chicken broth. Simmer 10 minutes. Add oysters and oyster liquid and then simmer an additional 5 minutes.

Remove lemon slices. If desired, thicken slightly with 1 to 2 tablespoons flour mixed to a thin paste with cold water, add a little hot liquid, and then stir into chowder. Serve with pilot crackers as a first course. ～

Pasta and Bean Soup

YIELD: 10 SERVINGS

1 tablespoon olive oil

1 cup chopped onions

1 cup chopped celery

1/2 cup chopped carrot

2 cloves garlic, minced

6 cups chicken broth

2 cups Northern beans, cooked

1 (15-ounce) can peeled, diced
   tomatoes, undrained

1 teaspoon dried oregano

1 teaspoon dried basil

1/2 teaspoon pepper

2 bay leaves

3/4 cup uncooked small shell
   macaroni

1 cup shredded Swiss cheese

1/4 cup chopped fresh parsley

Heat oil in Dutch oven or stockpot over medium heat until hot. Add onions, celery, carrot, and garlic, stirring, for 4 minutes. Add broth, beans, tomatoes, oregano, basil, pepper, and bay leaves. Bring to a boil. Add macaroni and then reduce heat to medium. Cook 10 to 13 minutes until pasta and vegetables are tender. Remove bay leaves. Sprinkle each portion with cheese and fresh parsley. ∾

Potato-Spinach Soup

YIELD: 4 SERVINGS

1 small onion, grated

3 tablespoons olive oil

4 cups cold water

2 medium potatoes, diced

1 cup chopped spinach

1 teaspoon salt

1/8 teaspoon pepper

1 cup milk

A little light cream

Sauté grated onion in olive oil until slightly yellow. Add 4 cups water, potatoes, spinach, salt, and pepper. Cook until potatoes are soft. Add milk and cream. Heat very hot, but do not boil. Serve with croutons. ∾

Provincetown Quahog Chowder

¼ cup salt pork, diced

¼ cup chopped onion

1 cup clam liquor and water

1 cup potatoes, diced

½ teaspoon salt

Dash pepper

3 quarts quahogs (hard-shell clams), shucked and chopped with liquid reserved

2 cups milk

Fry salt pork until golden. Add onion and cook until tender and transparent. Add liquor, potatoes, salt, pepper, and clams. Cook about 15 minutes or until potatoes are tender. Add milk. Heat. Serve with large pilot crackers. ∾

Rich Scallop Soup

YIELD: 6 SERVINGS

2 cups milk

1 cup heavy cream

2 tablespoons butter

1 teaspoon salt

1/4 teaspoon white pepper

1 teaspoon Worcestershire sauce

1 pound scallops, chopped into
 small pieces

3 tablespoons finely chopped
 fresh parsley

Paprika

In the top of a double boiler, blend milk, cream, butter, salt, pepper, and Worcestershire sauce. Place top of double boiler over the bottom with boiling water and bring to a simmer, stirring frequently. Add scallops to the mixture and cook until tender, about 8 to 10 minutes. Pour hot soup into individual bowls. Sprinkle each serving with parsley and paprika.

Spicy Crab Soup

YIELD: 8 SERVINGS

1 small, whole chicken, cut up

1 quart water

3 pounds canned tomatoes, quartered

8 ounces frozen corn, thawed

1 cup frozen peas, thawed

1 cup diced potatoes

3/4 cup diced celery

3/4 tablespoon seafood seasoning

1 teaspoon salt

1/4 teaspoon lemon pepper

1 pound fresh crabmeat, cartilage removed

Place chicken pieces in 6-quart stockpot and cover with water. This will make the chicken stock needed for the soup. Cover and simmer over low heat for at least 1 hour. Remove chicken pieces from stock. Add vegetables and seasonings to stock and simmer over low heat for 15 to 20 minutes. Add crabmeat and simmer for 15 minutes, until thoroughly heated. (If a milder soup is desired, decrease the amount of seafood seasoning to 1 1/2 teaspoons.)

Buzzards Bay fire apparatus, Buzzards Bay

Sweet Potato Stew

YIELD: TWO 1 1/2-CUP SERVINGS

2 teaspoons olive oil

1 medium onion, chopped

1 (15-ounce) can garbanzo beans, drained and rinsed

4 medium sweet potatoes, cooked and cut into 1/2-inch cubes

1/2 cup coarsely chopped dates

1/4 teaspoon turmeric

1 cup vegetable broth

1 tablespoon honey

2 tablespoons chopped, shelled pistachios

Heat oil in medium saucepan over medium heat until hot. Add onion and cook 3 to 5 minutes or until tender, stirring constantly.

Mix in all remaining ingredients except the pistachios and bring to a boil. Reduce heat and simmer 10 minutes or until thoroughly heated, stirring occasionally. Sprinkle each serving with pistachios.

Wellfleet Fish Chowder

YIELD: 8 SERVINGS

2 pounds fresh haddock

3 cups cold water

$1/4$ pound fat salt pork, diced into $1/4$-inch cubes

6 medium onions, finely chopped or sliced

4 medium potatoes, diced into $1/2$-inch cubes, or enough to make 2 cups

4 cups milk, heated but not boiled

Salt and pepper to taste

3 tablespoons butter

Cover haddock with the cold water and bring to a boil. Cook until just tender and fish begins to break apart. Remove fish from water, saving the cooking broth. Let cool. Fry salt pork until brown and crisp. Add onions and cook until soft. Add broth and potatoes, and simmer until potatoes are done. Add fish in chunks. Add milk, and salt and pepper to taste. Add butter and remove from heat. Cool 1 to 2 hours. Reheat just to boiling point before serving, without stirring, so the fish will remain in chunks. ∽

Winter Squash Soup

2 butternut squash, split, with seeds and stringy center removed

2 tablespoons olive oil

2 tablespoons minced garlic

1 tablespoon dried Italian herbs

Salt and pepper to taste

4 to 6 cups chicken stock

1/4 cup dry vermouth

Preheat oven to 350°F. Rub inside of squash with oil and garlic. Sprinkle with herbs and salt and pepper. Roast squash for 20 to 25 minutes, or until it is cooked. Remove from oven and let cool. Remove flesh from shells and mash or puree. Place in stockpot, add chicken stock, stir, and bring to a simmer. Add vermouth and serve with your favorite hearty bread and butter.

Railroad station, Hyannis

Fish

Assaduras de Peixe (Portuguese Fish Kabobs)

YIELD: 8 SERVINGS

4 cloves garlic, crushed

1 teaspoon crushed red pepper

1 teaspoon paprika

1 tablespoon salt

1 cup red wine vinegar

2 cups water

2 bay leaves, crushed

4 to 5 pounds pollock, cod, or
   haddock fillets

Combine all ingredients except fish to make a marinade called Vinha de Alhos. Pour over fillets. Marinate overnight. Drain fish, saving marinade. Cut fillets into long strips about 1 inch wide. Wind onto skewers, making loops in opposite directions, running skewer through fish at each turn. Place on broiler pan, about 4 inches from flame. Broil for 15 minutes, turning often and brushing with marinade, until fish flakes easily with a fork and is golden brown. ᴖ

Betty's Salmon

4 salmon fillets, 4 to 6 ounces each

2 tablespoons butter, melted

2 teaspoons soy sauce

2 teaspoons lemon juice

1 tablespoon snipped, fresh chives

1 tablespoon snipped parsley

1/4 teaspoon garlic powder

1/4 teaspoon onion powder

1/8 teaspoon pepper

Preheat oven to 350°F. Create a baking pan from a piece of heavy-duty foil by folding up approximately 1 inch on all sides and crimping the corners. Place the foil on an ungreased baking pan or cookie sheet. Place the salmon fillets on the foil. Cut 6 or 7 slashes in each fillet to allow for better penetration of seasonings.

In a small bowl, combine the remaining ingredients. Brush the butter mixture on the salmon fillets. Bake, uncovered, for 15 to 20 minutes, or until fish flakes easily when tested with a fork. ∼

Bluefish Alfredo

YIELD: 6 SERVINGS

2 pounds bluefish fillets, cut into 12 strips

1 cup white wine

3/4 teaspoon salt

1/2 teaspoon lemon pepper

1 teaspoon oregano

3/4 cup finely chopped fresh parsley

1/2 cup crushed almonds

12 cherry tomatoes

3 cups cooked medium egg noodles

1/4 cup Romano cheese

1 tablespoon olive oil

Pinch lemon pepper

Preheat oven to 400°F. Soak fish strips in wine for 5 to 10 minutes in the refrigerator. In a small bowl, mix together spices, 1/2 cup parsley, and almonds. Dip fish strips in mixture and then roll each piece around a cherry tomato. Place rolls on a lightly oiled baking dish. Bake for 10 to 14 minutes.

While fish is baking, prepare noodles according to package directions. Drain, and add 1/4 cup parsley, cheese, oil, and pepper. Place fish rolls on bed of noodles and serve immediately. ～

Broiled Mustard Dill Salmon

YIELD: 2 SERVINGS

1 pound fresh salmon fillet

1 lemon

2 tablespoons stone ground
  mustard

1 tablespoon minced fresh dill

Preheat broiler. Set rack 4 to 5 inches from flame or broiler element. Rinse fish in cold running water and pat dry. Place fillet skin side down on a baking sheet. With a zester or grater, remove zest from lemon. Mix lemon zest, lemon juice, mustard, and dill and brush mixture over fillet. Broil salmon until opaque in center, about 5 to 6 minutes for $1/2$-inch thick fillet or 10 to 12 minutes for 1-inch thick fillet. ✎

Cioppino Fish and Shellfish

YIELD: 8 SERVINGS

2 pounds striped bass or other flaky fish, cleaned, boned, and cut into 2-inch pieces

1 pint raw clams

1 pint raw oysters

1 pound small shrimp, cooked and cleaned

1 pound cooked crabmeat

1 pint bay scallops, raw

Four 1½ pound lobsters, boiled, split, and claws cracked

32 littleneck clams in shells, well-scrubbed, but not cooked

16 oysters in shell (cleaned but not cooked)

Preheat oven to 375°F. Layer the fish, clams, oysters, shrimp, crabmeat, and scallops in 8 well-buttered individual casseroles. Place ½ lobster and 1 claw on top of each. Tuck 4 little-neck clams and 2 oysters around the edge in each dish. Cover with a generous portion of the Cioppino Sauce (see page 13). Bake for 30 minutes, or until shellfish have opened. Serve with tossed salad and garlic toast.

Cod España

YIELD: 4 SERVINGS

1 tablespoon olive oil

1 pound cod fillets

1/4 teaspoon salt

3/4 teaspoon garlic-pepper blend

1/2 teaspoon dried oregano

1 tomato, sliced

1 small green pepper, cut into
   rings

1/2 lemon, sliced

Heat oil in large, nonstick skillet over medium-high heat until hot. If necessary, cut cod to fit in skillet. Sprinkle cod with salt and place in skillet. Cook 2 to 3 minutes or until lightly browned, turning once.

Sprinkle cod with garlic-pepper blend and oregano. Top with tomato and pepper slices. Arrange lemon slices around inside edge of skillet. Reduce heat to medium low, cover, and cook 10 to 12 minutes, or until fish flakes easily with a fork and vegetables are tender. If skillet becomes dry, add 1 to 2 tablespoons water.

Cranberry picking, Cape Cod

Cuttyhunk Swordfish Steaks

YIELD: 6 SERVINGS

2 pounds swordfish steaks, cut
about 1 inch thick

$^1/_3$ cup butter

$1^1/_2$ tablespoons flour

$^1/_4$ teaspoon salt

Few drops hot sauce

$^3/_4$ cup white wine

$^3/_4$ cup whipping cream

1 tablespoon lemon juice

Sugar to taste

1 cup seeded, halved white
grapes

Small bunch whole white
seedless grapes

Fresh sprigs of watercress

Brown swordfish steaks on both sides in $^1/_4$ cup of the butter. Cover and cook 10 minutes, or until fish flakes easily with a fork, but is still moist. Meanwhile, melt remaining butter and blend in flour, salt, and hot sauce. Add wine and cream. Stir over low heat until smooth and thickened. Cook 5 minutes longer. Remove from heat. Stir in lemon juice and a little sugar to taste. Add grapes and serve with the sauce over the steaks. Garnish with whole grapes and sprigs of watercress.

Deviled Scrod

YIELD: 4 SERVINGS

1¹/₂ to 2 pounds fresh scrod

¹/₄ cup chopped green pepper

¹/₄ cup minced onion

1 tablespoon Dijon mustard

1 teaspoon Worcestershire sauce

¹/₄ teaspoon hot sauce

3¹/₂ tablespoons lemon juice

¹/₂ cup butter

2 cups fine soft breadcrumbs

Salt and pepper to taste

2 tablespoons grated Parmesan cheese

Wipe scrod with a damp cloth and cut into 4 portions. Combine green pepper, onion, mustard, Worcestershire sauce, hot sauce, and lemon juice.

Melt butter and stir in breadcrumbs; add to vegetable mixture, blending well. Season scrod with salt and pepper and dot with additional butter. Place on foil-lined broiler rack with surface about 4 inches below source of heat. Broil for 5 minutes. Remove from broiler. Turn scrod and top with bread mixture. Return to broiler and broil 5 to 7 minutes, or until fish flakes easily with a fork. Sprinkle with Parmesan cheese. Broil 1 minute longer. ∾

Grilled Seafood Niçoise

YIELD: 4 SERVINGS

1^1/$_4$ cups prepared Italian salad
  dressing

2 medium potatoes, cooked,
  peeled, and sliced

^{1}/$_2$ pound (1^1/$_2$ cups) cut green
  beans, cooked and drained

1^1/$_2$ pounds fresh tuna steak,
  cuts into 1^1/$_2$-inch chunks

^{1}/$_2$ pound fresh sea scallops

Lettuce leaves

1 tomato, cut into 8 wedges

2 eggs, hard cooked, quartered

^{1}/$_4$ cup pitted ripe olives,
  quartered

In medium bowl, pour ^{1}/$_4$ cup dressing over potatoes and toss to cover. Cover and refrigerate 1 to 2 hours. In small bowl, pour 2 tablespoons dressing over green beans, tossing to coat. Cover and refrigerate 1 to 2 hours. In medium bowl, combine tuna, scallops, and ^{1}/$_2$ cup dressing. Cover bowl and refrigerate 1 to 2 hours.

Drain tuna and scallops, reserving marinade. Thread tuna and scallops on four 12- to 14-inch metal skewers and place on oiled broiler pan 4 inches from heat or on grill 4 to 6 inches from medium coals. Cook for 6 to 10 minutes, until fish flakes easily with a fork and scallops turn opaque, turning once and brushing frequently with marinade.

To serve, line large serving platter with lettuce. Spoon potatoes onto center of plate. Arrange tuna and scallops over potatoes. Spoon green beans around potatoes. Alternately place eggs and tomatoes over beans. Garnish with olives. Pour remaining dressing over salad. ∾

Macadamia Crusted Catfish

YIELD: 4 SERVINGS

2 skinless catfish fillets

2 cups lemon flavored yogurt

Tabasco sauce to taste

4 to 6 ounces macadamia nuts

1 cup plain breadcrumbs

1 cup cornmeal

1 tablespoon garlic seasoning

Canola oil for frying

Slice the fillets into 1-inch wide strips. Mix together yogurt and Tabasco sauce and marinate fish strips in this mixture for 1 hour. In a food processor fitted with a steel blade, process the macadamia nuts until ground. Add crumbs, cornmeal, and seasoning and process to combine. Roll strips in crumbs to coat.

Heat $1/2$-inch layer of oil in a deep pan over medium-high heat and fry fish strips in batches until golden brown and crispy, turning once, about 4 minutes per side. Drain on a paper towel-lined tray and keep warm while frying remainder of fish. Serve with tartar sauce. ❧

Mako Shark with Snow Peas

YIELD: 6 SERVINGS

3/4 cup white wine

3 tablespoons lemon juice

1 tablespoon Worcestershire sauce

2 pounds mako shark fillets, cut in 2-inch × 1-inch pieces

2/3 cup walnuts, finely chopped

1/4 cup minced onion

2/3 cup minced celery

1/4 cup dry parsley

1/4 cup breadcrumbs

1/4 teaspoon seafood seasoning

1/4 teaspoon salt

1/8 teaspoon lemon pepper

Paprika, for garnish

2 teaspoons oil

2 (10-ounce) packages frozen snow peas (pea pods)

1/2 cup water

Mix together wine, lemon juice, and Worcestershire sauce. Place fillets in a shallow dish and pour mixture evenly over fish. Marinate fish in refrigerator for 1/2 hour. In a medium bowl, combine walnuts, onion, celery, parsley, breadcrumbs, seafood seasoning, salt, and lemon pepper. Spread a thin layer of the walnut mixture over each fillet. Sprinkle with paprika. Discard marinade.

Preheat oven to 400°F. Lightly oil baking pan and place fillets on it. Bake for 10 to 15 minutes until fish is flaky and moist. While fish is baking, place frozen pea pods in a saucepan with 1/2 cup water. Add salt and pepper to taste. Cook just until hot. Do not overcook. Serve fish on a bed of pea pods.

Nantucket Flounder Rollups

YIELD: 6 TO 8 SERVINGS

12 large flounder fillets

8 strips bacon, diced

1/2 cup butter, melted

6 cups cornbread crumbs

1 teaspoon dried chervil

1 teaspoon dried tarragon leaves

Hot water

Butter

Preheat oven to 375°F. Cook bacon until crisp. Drain on absorbent paper, reserving bacon drippings. Measure 1/4 cup drippings and add to melted butter. Combine cornbread crumbs, bacon, herbs, and combined fats and mix well. Add enough hot water to make stuffing as moist as desired.

Place spoonful of stuffing on each flounder fillet and roll up firmly. Line baking pan with foil. Grease foil. Place rollups in pan and dot generously with butter. Bake for 25 minutes, or until fish flakes easily with a fork. Serve with the sauce of your choice. ∿

Oven-Fried Cod Fish

Y I E L D : 4 T O 6 S E R V I N G S

2 pounds fresh cod fillets

1 tablespoon salt

1 cup milk

1 cup breadcrumbs

4 tablespoons butter

Preheat oven to 500°F. Cut fillets into serving-sized pieces. Add salt to milk and mix. Dip fish in milk and roll in breadcrumbs. Place in well-oiled baking pan and pour melted butter over fish. Place pan on top shelf of hot oven and bake 10 to 12 minutes, or until fish flakes easily with a fork. Serve immediately on a hot platter. ⌒

Pan-Fried Sole

YIELD: 2 SERVINGS

1 pound fresh sole fillets

Salt and pepper to taste

1/2 cup fine dry breadcrumbs

1/2 teaspoon paprika

1 lemon

1 tablespoon olive oil

Rinse fish and pat dry. Cut fillets to fit frying pan, if needed. Lightly season fillets with salt and pepper. Combine breadcrumbs and paprika. Dip fillets in crumb mixture and turn to thoroughly coat, shaking off excess. Squeeze juice from half the lemon and cut remaining half into wedges.

Heat oil in frying pan (preferably a nonstick pan) over medium-high heat. Lay fish in pan without overlapping and cook until edges turn opaque and bottom is browned, 2 to 3 minutes. Carefully turn and cook until opaque through center, 1 to 2 minutes more. Transfer fish to plates and cover to keep warm. Add lemon juice to pan and boil to thicken, about 30 seconds, scraping up cooked bits. Pour sauce over fish and garnish with lemon wedges. ∾

New Central House, Provincetown

Peppered Salmon with Dill-Caper Sauce

YIELD: 1 SERVING

$^1/_2$ pound salmon fillet

$^1/_4$ teaspoon Dijon mustard

$^3/_4$ teaspoon course ground pepper

$^1/_2$ teaspoon mustard seed

1 tablespoon capers

1 teaspoon chopped fresh dill, or $^1/_4$ teaspoon dried dill weed

2 tablespoons sour cream

2 teaspoons mayonnaise

1 teaspoon milk

2 or 3 drops hot pepper sauce

Lemon slices or wedges, for garnish

Sourdough bread slices

Place salmon skin side down on work surface. Spread top surface with mustard. In small bowl, combine pepper and mustard seed and mix well. Sprinkle over mustard and press into salmon.

To grill salmon, place salmon skin side down on gas grill over medium heat or on charcoal grill 4 to 6 inches over medium coals. To broil salmon, place skin side down on broiler pan and broil 4 to 6 inches from heat for 10 to 12 minutes, or until fish flakes easily with a fork.

Meanwhile, in small bowl, combine all ingredients except lemon and bread, blending well. Carefully remove skin from cooked salmon, leaving salmon in 1 piece. Place on serving plate, mustard side up. Garnish plate with lemon slices or wedges. Serve with sauce and sourdough bread slices. ∾

Poached Fish in Wine with Grapes

YIELD: 2 SERVINGS

1 small onion, sliced thin

1 tablespoon olive oil

2 small potatoes, sliced thin

3/4 cup good white wine

1/4 cup water

1 pound fresh cod

1 small bunch seedless white grapes (4 to 6 ounces)

1/2 teaspoon salt

Fresh ground black pepper to taste

Sauté onion in olive oil. Add potatoes, wine, and water. Place fish on top and spread grapes around the sides. Season with salt and pepper. Cover and poach over low heat until potatoes are tender, fish flakes easily, and the grapes are soft. ❧

Portugesa Calamari

1 pound squid, cleaned and cut into 3/4-inch rings

1 medium onion

2 garlic cloves, minced

4 tablespoons olive oil

1/4 teaspoon sugar

4 shakes crushed red pepper

Salt to taste

2 bay leaves

2 tablespoons chopped fresh parsley

8 whole tomatoes, cut up

1/2 cup red wine

6 medium boiled potatoes, quartered

In a 2-quart saucepan, sauté squid, onion, and garlic for 5 minutes. Add remaining ingredients except for wine and potatoes and simmer for 30 minutes on medium-high heat. Add wine and simmer over low heat for 30 to 40 minutes more. Sauce should be medium thick. Serve over boiled potatoes. ~

Red Snapper with Orange Sauce

YIELD: 6 SERVINGS

Red Snapper:

1 1/2 red snapper fillets

1/4 teaspoon salt

1/8 teaspoon pepper

1/2 to 1 teaspoon minced garlic

1 tablespoon butter

1 teaspoon grated orange peel

3 tablespoons orange juice

Orange Sauce:

1 whole clove garlic

2 tablespoons butter

3 tablespoons orange juice

1/8 teaspoon ground ginger

2 tablespoons snipped parsley

Preheat the oven to 400°F. In a large baking pan, arrange the red snapper fillets in a single layer. Sprinkle the fillets with salt and pepper.

In a small saucepan, cook the minced garlic in the butter for about 30 seconds over medium heat. Sprinkle garlic-butter mixture, grated orange peel, and orange juice over the fillets.

Bake the fillets, uncovered, until the fish flakes easily when tested with a fork. (Allow 4 to 6 minutes per 1/2-inch thickness of fish.) Transfer the fillets to a platter and keep warm.

Meanwhile, make the orange sauce. In a small saucepan over medium heat, cook the garlic clove in butter until the garlic begins to turn golden. Remove and discard the garlic clove. Stir in orange juice and ginger. To serve, spoon some of the sauce over each fillet and sprinkle with parsley. ∾

Salmon with Dill Sauce

YIELD: 4 SERVINGS

8 ounces plain yogurt

2 tablespoons chopped green
   onions

1/2 teaspoon grated lemon peel

1 teaspoon dried dill weed

4 cups water

1 small onion, sliced

1 lemon, sliced

4 to 6 peppercorns

4 (4-ounce) salmon steaks or
   fillets

To prepare sauce, combine yogurt, green onions, lemon peel, and dill weed in a small bowl. Blend well, cover, and refrigerate until serving time.

In a large skillet, combine water, onion, lemon, and peppercorns. Bring to a boil, reduce heat, and simmer 5 minutes to blend flavors. Add salmon and simmer 7 to 10 minutes, or until salmon flakes easily with a fork. Remove from heat. Lift salmon carefully with a slotted spoon or spatula. Serve with yogurt dill sauce. ∾

Salmon with Sour Cream-Mustard Topping

YIELD: 1 SERVING

1 (6-ounce) salmon steak, 3/4 to
   1 inch thick

1 to 2 tablespoons butter, melted

1/8 teaspoon salt

Dash of pepper

2 tablespoons dairy sour cream

1 1/2 teaspoons Dijon mustard

1 teaspoon lemon juice

1/8 teaspoon dried dill weed

Place salmon steak on oiled broiler pan. Brush salmon with butter. Broil 4 to 6 inches from heat for 10 to 15 minutes, or until fish flakes easily with fork, turning and brushing with butter once during cooking. Sprinkle with salt and pepper.

In small bowl, combine sour cream, mustard, lemon juice, and dill weed, mixing well. Serve over fish.

Spicy Salmon Steaks

YIELD: 2 SERVINGS

2 salmon steaks, 6 to 8 ounces each, and 1 inch thick

1/2 medium green bell pepper

1/2 medium red bell pepper

1/2 teaspoon Worcestershire sauce

1/2 teaspoon lemon juice

1/4 teaspoon Cajun spice blend

Rinse fish and pat dry. Core, seed, and dice bell peppers. Arrange steaks side by side in a baking dish; press thin belly flaps together, and then press against body of other steak. Rub the top of each steak with 1/4 teaspoon Worcestershire sauce and 1/4 teaspoon lemon juice. Sprinkle or rub each steak with 1/8 teaspoon Cajun spice blend. Sprinkle diced bell peppers over top.

To microwave, cover dish tightly with plastic wrap and microwave on High (full power) until fish is nearly opaque, 5 to 6 minutes. Let stand, still covered, 1 to 2 minutes longer.

To bake, preheat oven to 375°F and bake, uncovered, 10 to 12 minutes, or until fish is opaque and flakes easily. ∾

Squid with Tomatoes (Calamari con Pomodore)

YIELD: 4 TO 6 SERVINGS

2 pounds squid

1/2 onion, minced

2 large garlic cloves

4 tablespoons olive oil

Salt and pepper to taste

1/2 cup dry sherry

Dried crushed oregano to taste

Dried crushed red pepper flakes
   to taste (optional)

1 cup tomatoes

2 tablespoons minced fresh
   parsley

Clean squid thoroughly. Remove outside skin, eyes, and intestines. Clean skin off tentacles and slice body into 1-inch rings. Sauté onion and garlic in olive oil. Add squid, cover, and sauté for 10 minutes. Add salt, pepper, sherry oregano, and red pepper flakes. Cook for 10 minutes more over low heat without cover to allow liquid to cook off. Add tomatoes (crushed between fingers) and parsley. Cook for another 20 minutes. ∾

Stuffed Flounder Fillets

YIELD: 8 SERVINGS

½ cup water

½ cup tomato juice

½ cup butter

1 cup (8 ounces) herb-seasoned
   bread stuffing mix

1 cup chopped, fresh raw
   hard-shell clams (quahaugs)

8 flounder fillets

Melted butter

Preheat oven to 400°F. Combine water and tomato juice and add butter. Heat until butter is melted. Add stuffing mix and clams with their juice, mixing well. Spread stuffing mix on 4 fillets. Top with remaining fillets and tie each pair securely with white string. Place in shallow baking dish, adding just enough hot water to barely cover bottom of fish. Brush tops of stuffed fillets with melted butter. Bake for 20 minutes, or until fish flakes easily with a fork. Serve with a dill relish tartar sauce. ∾

Trout Stuffed with Spinach

YIELD: 4 SERVINGS

5 garlic cloves, peeled and sliced

1/2 bunch baby spinach, rinsed
   and trimmed

Salt and pepper to taste

4 small trout, bones and scales
   removed

Flour

2 tablespoons butter

2 tablespoons olive oil

1 lemon, cut into 4 wedges

Blanch the garlic in boiling water for 3 minutes. Drain, rinse with cold water, and rinse again.

Wilt the spinach leaves in a Dutch oven over high heat, turning occasionally for 3 minutes. Remove from heat, squeeze out excess water, and chop coarsely. Combine in small bowl with garlic, salt, and pepper.

Season inside of trout with salt and pepper. Divide spinach mixture and tuck inside fish. Tie string around center to hold stuffing. Dust the outsides with flour and season with salt and pepper.

Preheat oven to 400°F. Melt butter and oil in 2 large skillets over high heat. Fry the fish about 1 minute per side. Transfer to hot oven and cook 4 minutes, turning after 2 minutes. Serve hot with lemon wedges.

Cape Cod fruit, Cape Cod

Shellfish

Baked Scallops

YIELD: 4 SERVINGS

2 tablespoons white wine

1 tablespoon lemon juice

$1/4$ teaspoon salt

$1/4$ teaspoon white pepper

1 pound bay or calico scallops,
   or 1 pound sea scallops,
   quartered

$1/4$ cup heavy cream

$1/2$ cup fresh breadcrumbs

2 tablespoons butter, melted

Preheat oven to 400°F. Mix wine, lemon juice, salt, and pepper in medium bowl. Stir in scallops. Add cream and stir. Place mixture in shallow baking dish. Mix breadcrumbs with butter and sprinkle over scallops. Bake until scallops are done, mixture is bubbly, and crumb topping is browned (approximately 15 minutes).

Baked Lobster Provincetown

YIELD: 2 LARGE SERVINGS

2 (2-pound) live lobsters

6 tablespoons butter

1/2 cup sliced fresh mushrooms

1/4 cup diced green pepper

2 tablespoons flour

1 cup milk

1/2 cup sherry

1 teaspoon paprika

Salt to taste

1 tablespoon diced pimiento

1/4 cup fresh breadcrumbs

1/4 cup mild grated cheese

Cook lobsters. To clean lobsters, cut off lobster claws and legs so that only body remains. Hold lobster with top side up. Using kitchen shears, cut an oval opening in the top of the shell, from the base of the head to the tail. Remove all the meat from the body and the claws. Cube meat.

Preheat oven to 375°F. Melt butter in 2-quart saucepan. Sauté mushrooms and green pepper in butter until tender. Blend in flour and add milk. Cook and stir until mixture comes to a boil and thickens. Add sherry, paprika, and salt. Simmer 5 minutes. Remove from heat. Add lobster meat and pimiento and mix well.

Pile filling into the 2 lobster shells. Sprinkle with breadcrumbs, gently pressing breadcrumbs into lobster mixture. Top with grated cheese. Bake until cheese melts and mixture is bubbly, about 15 minutes. ∾

Bay Crab Cakes

YIELD: 6 CAKES

1 pound blue crab meat, fresh

2 eggs

1/4 cup mayonnaise

1 teaspoon seafood seasoning

1/4 teaspoon white pepper

2 teaspoons Worcestershire sauce

1 teaspoon dry mustard

1 cup cracker crumbs

Carefully remove all cartilage from crabmeat. In a bowl, mix together remaining ingredients. Add crabmeat and mix evenly and gently. Add cracker crumbs evenly. Shape into 6 cakes and sauté in a frying pan in a little oil for 5 minutes on each side. ∾

Broiled Stuffed Lobster

YIELD: 4 SERVINGS

1 large lobster (3 to 3¹/₂ pounds),
    or 2 lobsters (2 pounds each)

1 pound bay scallops, or 1
    pound sea scallops, quartered

2 tablespoons butter

2 tablespoons flour

¹/₂ cup tomato sauce

¹/₂ cup whipping cream

1 teaspoon chervil

¹/₂ teaspoon tarragon

Salt and pepper to taste

3 egg yolks, well beaten

³/₄ cup buttered crumbs

Plunge lobsters into large amount of boiling, salted water. Cover. Simmer 5 minutes for the first pound and 3 minutes for each additional pound. Remove lobster. Place on its back and split in half from end to end, starting at the head. Remove stomach and intestinal vein. Reserve green liver (tomalley) and the coral (roe) if any is present. Leave claws intact. Remove tail meat and dice.

Meanwhile, simmer scallops for 5 minutes and drain, saving 1 cup of the stock. Melt butter, blend in flour, and add stock. Cook and stir over medium heat until thickened. Stir in tomato sauce, cream, chervil, and tarragon. Season with salt and pepper. Stir in egg yolks and simmer 3 minutes, stirring constantly. Add scallops and diced lobster meat. Fill body cavity and tail of lobster with this mixture. Top with buttered crumbs. Broil just until crumbs brown and mixture is bubbling hot. Claws may be cracked and the meat served at the table, or they may be saved for another meal. ❧

Cape Shore Crab Cakes

1/4 cup butter

1 medium onion, chopped

1/4 cup snipped parsley

1/2 cup flour

1 cup milk

2 eggs

12 to 16 ounces fresh crabmeat

1/4 teaspoon salt

1/8 teaspoon pepper

3 eggs, beaten

1 cup cracker crumbs

1/4 cup vegetable oil

In a large skillet, melt the butter. Add the onion and parsley and cook until tender. Add the flour and stir until blended.

In a small bowl, beat together the milk and 2 eggs. Add to the hot mixture. Cook, stirring constantly, until the mixture is thick and coming away from the sides of the pan. Add the crabmeat and mix well. Season with salt and pepper. Let cool.

Form the mixture into 8 to 12 flat cakes, 1/2 to 3/4 inch thick. Dip the cakes into the 3 beaten eggs and roll in cracker crumbs.

In a large skillet, fry the crab cakes in hot oil over medium heat, about 2 minutes per side, or until golden brown. Using a slotted spatula, remove the crab cakes from the pan and drain on paper towels. ✑

Deviled Crabs

YIELD: 6 SERVINGS

6 large scallop shells

1½ cups fresh crabmeat

5 tablespoons butter

1½ tablespoons flour

¾ cup light cream

2 eggs, beaten

½ teaspoon salt

1½ teaspoons prepared mustard

½ teaspoon paprika

⅛ teaspoon cayenne

Wash and dry scallop shells. Flake crabmeat and remove any cartilage. Melt 1 tablespoon butter in a saucepan. Add flour and cream. Cook over low heat until thickened. Remove from heat. Add eggs, salt, mustard, paprika, and cayenne. Stir ingredients until thoroughly blended. Add crabmeat and mix well. Pack into scallop shells. Melt remaining butter and pour over filled shells. Brown quickly under broiler and serve bubbly hot.

shavings shop, Chatham

Eastport Lobster Casserole

YIELD: 4 TO 6 SERVINGS

3/4 to 1 pound lobster meat

3 tablespoons butter

3 tablespoons flour

3/4 teaspoon dry mustard

Salt and pepper to taste

1 cup heavy cream

1/2 cup milk

1/4 cup sherry

2 to 3 slices French bread, crusts removed

Cut lobster meat into bite-sized pieces and cook slowly in butter. Do not overcook or cook too fast, as lobster will then become tough. Remove lobster meat and add flour mixed with seasonings to butter in pan. Add cream and milk slowly. Cook, stirring constantly over low heat, until thickened. Add sherry, lobster meat, and bread torn into small pieces. Pour into oiled casserole. Top with a few buttered crumbs. If desired, you may add a small amount of cooked crabmeat and/or shrimp before baking. Cook for 30 minutes at 350°F.

Garlic Broiled Shrimp

2 pounds raw shrimp

1/2 cup olive oil

1/4 wine vinegar

1 tablespoon snipped parsley

1/2 teaspoon oregano

1/2 teaspoon salt

1/4 teaspoon black pepper

12 cloves garlic, minced

Shell and devein shrimp. Combine remaining ingredients in a 2-quart mixing bowl. Add shrimp. Marinate for several hours, turning shrimp several times. Drain shrimp and place on preheated broiler with rack in low position. Broil about 3 minutes on each side.

Hyannisport Lobster Pie

YIELD: 4 SERVINGS

3/4 cup butter

1/2 cup sherry

2 cups cut-up cooked lobster
meat

2 tablespoons flour

1/2 teaspoon salt

1 1/2 cups light cream

4 egg yolks

1/2 cup cracker meal

1 teaspoon paprika

3 tablespoons crushed potato
chips

2 tablespoons grated Parmesan
cheese

Preheat oven to 300°F. In a sauté pan, melt 1/4 cup butter. Add sherry and boil for 2 minutes. Remove from heat and add lobster meat.

Melt 1/4 cup butter in top of double boiler. Stir in flour and salt. Add cream and the sherry mixture, drained from lobster. Cook, stirring, until thickened. Beat egg yolks and gradually add to hot sauce, stirring continuously. Return to heat and cook over simmering water about 3 minutes. Remove from heat. Add lobster and place in 4 individual baking dishes. Mix remaining ingredients with 1/4 cup melted butter and sprinkle over top. Bake about 15 minutes, or until thoroughly heated. ～

Lobster Supreme

8 tablespoons butter

6 tablespoons flour

1^1/$_2$ cups milk

^{1}/$_2$ cup dry sherry

8 drops Worcestershire sauce

^{1}/$_2$ teaspoon lemon pepper
seasoning

Salt to taste

3 green onions, minced
(about ^{1}/$_4$ cup)

6 sliced mushrooms

3 cups cooked lobster meat, cut
into bite-sized pieces

Paprika, for sprinkling

In 3-quart saucepan, melt 6 tablespoons butter. Mix in flour. Slowly add milk, stirring constantly to keep mixture smooth and free from lumps. Cook, stirring, over medium heat, until mixture comes to a boil and thickens. Add sherry, Worcestershire sauce, lemon pepper, and salt. Simmer 2 minutes.

In another pan, sauté green onions and mushrooms in 2 tablespoons butter, until green onions are tender. Add to sauce mixture. Gently stir lobster meat into sauce mixture.

Preheat oven to 450°F. Put mixture into individual shells or ramekins (or greased 2-quart casserole). Sprinkle paprika over top. Bake for 10 to 15 minutes, until hot and bubbly and lightly browned on top. ❧

Lobster in Whiskey Sauce

YIELD: 4 SERVINGS

3 fresh boiled lobsters

1 tablespoon butter

1 tablespoon flour

1 pint Lobster Bisque (see page 65)

4 ounces fresh thick cream

2 egg yolks

4 ounces Scotch whiskey

Salt and pepper to taste

Remove lobster meat from shells, keeping chunks as big as possible. Melt butter in small saucepan, add the flour, and cook for about 1 minute. Add the lobster bisque, stirring continuously, and cook the sauce for 1 to 2 minutes longer. Cover and remove from heat, keeping the sauce warm.

Whip the cream until stiff. Add in the well-beaten egg yolks and mix well. At the last moment, place the lobster meat in a preheated tray (covered). Add the whiskey to the sauce. Stir the cream mixture through the sauce. Season with salt and pepper. Pour over the lobster. Serve with cooked rice. ✌

Oyster Corn Fritters

YIELD: ABOUT 2 DOZEN FRITTERS

1 egg

1 pint shucked oysters, drained, and liquor reserved

2 cups all-purpose biscuit mix

$1/4$ teaspoon seafood seasoning

$1/8$ teaspoon salt

$1/8$ teaspoon lemon and pepper seasoning

1 cup whole kernel corn, drained

Vegetable oil for frying

In large bowl, beat egg slightly. Add water to oyster liquor to make $3/4$ cup liquid. Add liquid and biscuit mix to eggs, blending well. Mix in seasonings. Gently stir in corn and oysters.

In large frying pan, heat 1 to 2 inches oil to 350°F. Drop batter into hot oil by tablespoonful, making sure to include 1 oyster in each portion. Cook until brown on 1 side, 1 to 2 minutes. Turn and brown the other side. ∽

Provincetown Crab Cakes

YIELD: 6 CAKES

1 pound crabmeat

1 egg

1/4 cup finely chopped green
    pepper

1 slice white bread, cubed

1 teaspoon Worcestershire sauce

1 teaspoon dry mustard

1 teaspoon lemon juice

1/2 teaspoon salt

1/4 teaspoon pepper

Vegetable oil for frying

Remove cartilage from crabmeat. In medium bowl, beat egg slightly. Add remaining ingredients and crabmeat and mix gently but thoroughly. Shape into 6 cakes.

Cook in frying pan in just enough oil to prevent sticking, until browned, for about 5 minutes on each side. ∽

Sagamore Shrimp Pie

4 slices white bread, crumbled

3/4 cup sherry (or a little less)

1 green pepper

1 pound shrimp or lobster

2 hard-boiled eggs

4 tablespoons butter

1/2 pint sour cream

Pinch of nutmeg

Salt and pepper to taste

Preheat oven to 350°F. Soak the bread in sherry. In a frying pan, sauté green pepper in butter. Mix all ingredients and place in buttered casserole. Bake for 30 minutes.

Artist Beach, Provincetown

Scallops New England

1/2 cup butter

5 tablespoons raw minced spinach

2 tablespoons minced clams

3 tablespoons minced lettuce

2 tablespoons minced celery

3 tablespoons fine dry breadcrumbs

1/4 teaspoon herb-blend for fish

1/2 teaspoon anchovy paste

Pepper

1/4 teaspoon salt

36 sea scallops (about 3 pounds)

In a large frying pan, melt 5 tablespoons butter. Add all remaining ingredients except scallops and mix well. Heat gently, making sure that the butter does not brown.

Place scallops on foil-lined broiler pan and dot with remaining butter. Broil until lightly browned. Place 6 scallops in each of 6 scallop shells. Scatter spinach mixture over all. Broil until thoroughly heated. Serve immediately. ❧

Scallops Portuguese

YIELD: 8 SERVINGS

1 pound cape scallops, or 1
   pound sea scallops (cut in half)

¼ cup butter

3 large garlic cloves, minced

½ teaspoon salt

Freshly ground black pepper

½ cup chopped fresh parsley

Pat scallops dry with paper towel. In a frying pan, melt butter. Add garlic and salt and cook until garlic is golden. Add scallops and cook 5 to 7 minutes, stirring often. Sprinkle with pepper. Add parsley and cook 1 minute longer. Serve hot. ∾

Simple Shrimp Creole

YIELD: 4 SERVINGS

2 tablespoons butter

1/2 cup finely chopped onion

2 tablespoons flour

3 cups water

1 (6-ounce) can tomato paste

1/2 cup finely chopped green
pepper

1/4 cup finely chopped celery

1 teaspoon snipped fresh parsley

1/2 teaspoon salt

1/4 teaspoon bottled hot pepper
sauce

Dash to 1/4 teaspoon ground red
pepper

1 bay leaf

2 cups cooked shrimp

2 cups hot cooked rice

In a large heavy skillet over medium heat, melt the butter. Add the onion and cook until tender, but not brown. Stir in the flour. Add the water, tomato paste, green pepper, celery, parsley, salt, hot pepper sauce, ground red pepper, and bay leaf. Cook, uncovered, over medium low heat for about 30 minutes, or until thickened, stirring occasionally. Stir in the shrimp and heat through. Remove the bay leaf. Serve over the hot, cooked rice. ∿

Summer Sea Bass, Shrimp, and Scallop Pie

YIELD: 8 SERVINGS

1 small onion

1 carrot

1 stalk celery

Salt and pepper to taste

4 cups water

$1^{1}/_{2}$ pounds sea bass, cut into chunks

1 cup chicken stock

2 tablespoons butter

1 tablespoon chopped onion

2 tablespoons flour

1 teaspoon chopped parsley

$^{1}/_{2}$ pound boiled shrimp

$^{1}/_{2}$ pound boiled scallops

$^{1}/_{2}$ recipe of your favorite pie crust

Boil onion, carrot, and celery with salt, pepper, shrimp, and scallops for 10 minutes in water. Remove shrimp and scallops. Wrap bass in cheesecloth, add to boiling water, and simmer, covered, until tender. Take fish from water, remove skin and bones, place on hot plate. Return skin and bones to stock, add chicken stock, and cook 15 minutes longer. Strain and reserve stock.

Preheat oven to 450°F. Melt butter in a skillet. Add chopped onion and sauté over low heat until onion is tender. Slowly add flour, stirring until smooth. Blend in $2^{1}/_{4}$ cups strained fish stock. Add parsley and salt and pepper to taste.

Alternate layers of fish, shrimp, and scallops in deep, well-greased baking dish. Pour the sauce over all and cover with rolled-out pie crust. Cut several vents in crust with a sharp knife. Bake in 450°F oven 12 minutes. Reduce heat to 350°F and bake 20 minutes longer.

Mill built in 1774, Chatham

Poultry

Apple Honey-Glazed Chicken

YIELD: 4 SERVINGS

1/3 cup apple jelly

1 tablespoon honey

1 tablespoon Dijon mustard

1/2 teaspoon cinnamon

1/2 teaspoon salt

4 boneless, skinless chicken
    breast halves

To barbecue, heat grill. In small bowl, combine all ingredients except chicken and blend well. When ready to barbecue, oil grill rack. Brush chicken with jelly mixture. Place on gas grill over medium heat or on charcoal grill 4 to 6 inches from medium coals. Cook 15 to 20 minutes, or until chicken is fork tender and juices run clear, turning occasionally and brushing frequently with jelly mixture.

To broil, prepare jelly mixture as directed. Lightly grease broiler pan. Brush chicken with jelly mixture and place on greased broiler pan. Broil 4 to 6 inches from heat for 15 to 20 minutes, or until chicken is fork tender and juices run clear, turning occasionally and brushing frequently with jelly mixture. Discard any remaining jelly mixture.

Baked Chicken and Yams

YIELD: 4 TO 6 SERVINGS

1 (2½ pound) broiler/fryer
   chicken, quartered

½ teaspoon salt

¼ teaspoon pepper

2 eggs, beaten

3 tablespoons water

¾ cup fine, plain breadcrumbs

2 pounds yams or sweet
   potatoes, peeled and sliced
   ½ inch thick

⅓ cup butter, melted

Sprinkle the chicken quarters with salt and pepper. In a pie plate, stir together the eggs and water. In a second pie plate, spread the breadcrumbs.

One piece at a time, dip the chicken quarters first in the egg mixture and then in the breadcrumbs, patting to cover the chicken well. Keep the wet and dry mixtures separate by using one hand for the egg mixture and the other for the breadcrumbs.

Preheat oven to 350°F. Lightly grease a 13 × 9 × 2-inch baking pan. Place the yam slices in the prepared pan. Drizzle with half of the melted butter. Arrange the chicken on top of the yams. Drizzle the remaining butter over the chicken.

Bake the chicken, uncovered, for about 1 hour, or until the yams are tender and the chicken is cooked through. Arrange chicken and yams on a warm platter and serve at once.

Brandied Chicken

1 (2$^{1}/_{2}$ pound) chicken, cut for frying

2 cloves garlic

$^{1}/_{2}$ stick butter

1 cup heavy cream

2 jiggers brandy or rum

1 tablespoon curry powder

Salt and pepper to taste

Preheat oven to 350°F. In a frying pan, sauté the chicken and garlic in butter. Transfer to covered casserole with the juices. Add cream, brandy, curry, salt, and pepper. Cover and bake for 45 to 60 minutes. Serve with rice. ✎

Chicken and Zucchini with Garlic

YIELD: 4 SERVINGS

1/3 cup barbecue sauce

2 teaspoons vinegar

2 cloves garlic, minced

2 tablespoons oil

4 boneless chicken thighs

4 chicken drumsticks, skinned

2 medium zucchini, sliced and quartered, 1/4 inch thick (3 cups)

In small bowl, combine barbecue sauce, vinegar, and garlic and mix well. Set aside.

Heat oil in large skillet over medium-high heat until hot. Add chicken thighs and drumsticks. Cook 8 to 10 minutes, or until brown. Pour barbecue sauce mixture over chicken. Reduce heat, cover, and simmer 20 minutes, or until chicken is fork tender and juices run clear, turning chicken once halfway through cooking. Place chicken on serving platter and keep warm.

Drain sauce into small bowl, skimming off fat. Return 3 tablespoons of the sauce to skillet. Add zucchini and cook, stirring, over medium-high heat 3 minutes, or until lightly browned and crisp tender. Spoon zucchini onto serving platter with chicken. Serve with remaining sauce, if desired. ～

Chicken in Wine

YIELD: 6 TO 8 SERVINGS

2 broiler-fryer chickens (3 pounds each), cut into pieces

1/2 cup flour

1 1/2 teaspoons salt

1/2 cup olive oil

1/2 cup diced ham

10 small white onions

10 whole mushrooms

2 cloves garlic, minced

1/4 teaspoon freshly ground black pepper

1/4 teaspoon thyme

1 sprig parsley

1 bay leaf

1 1/2 cups dry red wine

Dredge chicken pieces in flour mixed with 1 teaspoon salt. Heat oil in 5-quart Dutch oven. Add a few pieces of chicken and brown on all sides. Remove chicken and brown a few more pieces until all is browned. Then return all the pieces to the Dutch oven. Add ham, onions, mushrooms, garlic, salt, pepper, thyme, parsley, and bay leaf. Add wine. Cover, reduce heat to low, and simmer for 1 1/2 hours, or until chicken is very tender. ✦

Citrus 'n Honey Chicken

2 (3- to 3½-pound) frying
   chickens, cut up, skinned if
   desired

1 teaspoon salt

¼ cup lemon juice

¼ cup orange juice

¼ cup honey

2 tablespoons oil

1 tablespoon prepared mustard

¼ teaspoon dried thyme

¼ teaspoon dried marjoram

Place chicken pieces in large saucepan or Dutch oven. Add salt and enough water to cover. Bring to a boil. Reduce heat, cover, and simmer for 10 minutes. Remove from heat and drain. In 12 × 8-inch (2-quart) glass baking dish or plastic bag, combine remaining ingredients and blend well. Add chicken, turning to coat. Cover dish or seal bag and refrigerate 2 to 4 hours, turning several times. Drain chicken, reserving marinade.

Preheat oven to 350°F. Line a 13 × 9-inch baking dish with foil. Place chicken in foil-lined dish and brush with marinade. Bake for 30 to 40 minutes, or until chicken is fork tender and juices run clear, brushing frequently with marinade. Discard any remaining marinade. ∾

Railroad station, Eastham

Grilled Sesame Chicken

YIELD: 4 SERVINGS

3 tablespoons soy sauce

1 cup pineapple juice

1 tablespoon grated fresh ginger

1 tablespoon sesame oil

1 clove garlic, crushed

1/4 cup sesame seeds

4 whole chicken breasts,
  without skin

Combine all ingredients except sesame seeds and chicken. Marinate chicken in refrigerator for 3 hours. Save marinade and simmer for about 3 to 5 minutes for basting sauce. Grill chicken, basting often, for approximately 8 minutes per side, depending on thickness. Toast sesame seeds on foil or dry skillet on grill, stirring often for an even golden brown. Sprinkle sesame seeds over chicken on plate and serve with grilled fresh vegetables. ❧

Maple-Glazed Chicken

YIELD: 6 SERVINGS

12 slices bacon

6 chicken quarters

1 cup whole berry cranberry
  sauce

1/2 cup maple syrup

Microwave bacon for 4 minutes on High, until bacon is partially cooked. Wrap 2 strips bacon around each chicken quarter. Place in a large baking pan. Combine cranberry sauce and maple syrup. Brush glaze on chicken.

Preheat oven to 350°F, and bake chicken for 1 hour 15 minutes, or until chicken is no longer pink inside, brushing frequently with glaze.

Whiskey Chicken Cutlets

6 to 8 boneless chicken cutlets

1/3 cup sweet paprika

1 tablespoon black pepper

1 tablespoon salt

1 tablespoon olive oil

1 teaspoon minced fresh garlic

1 bunch scallions, chopped

1 cup whiskey

2 cups chicken stock

2 tablespoons tomato paste

1 tablespoon honey

1/2 cup chopped fresh parsley

1/2 cup chopped fresh basil

2 tablespoons dried Italian herb blend

Preheat oven to 350°F. Dust chicken cutlets in sweet paprika, black pepper, and salt. Sear cutlets on both sides in a very hot, empty nonstick sauté pan. Place cutlets in a single layer in a baking dish and keep warm.

Heat the oil in the same pan in which the cutlets were seared and sauté the garlic and scallions. Add whiskey and chicken stock and simmer 10 minutes. Add remaining ingredients and simmer together for a few minutes more. Season to taste with salt and pepper. Pour mixture over chicken cutlets. Bake for 10 to 12 minutes until bubbly hot. ∾

Waterfront, Edgartown

Meats and Pasta

Apple Pork Tenderloin

1 teaspoon oil

1 pound pork tenderloins, cut into 1/4-inch slices

1/4 teaspoon salt (optional)

1/8 teaspoon pepper

2 ripe plums, pitted, sliced

1 large apple, unpeeled, sliced

1/2 cup apple cider

2 tablespoons brown sugar

2 teaspoons cornstarch

1 tablespoon water

Heat oil in large skillet over medium-high heat until hot. Add pork and sprinkle with salt and pepper. Cook 5 to 7 minutes, or until pork is tender and no longer pink. Add plums, apple, and cider. Cover and simmer 10 minutes, or until fruit is tender. Meanwhile, in small bowl, combine remaining ingredients; add to skillet. Cook over medium heat until mixture is thickened and bubbly, stirring constantly. Boil 1 minute. ~

Belgian Endives with Ham Au Gratin

YIELD: 3 TO 4 SERVINGS

1/2 cup butter

1/2 cup lemon juice

2 tablespoons water

1 teaspoon salt

6 to 8 Belgian endives, roots trimmed

1/4 teaspoon flour

Dash cayenne pepper

2 cups milk

3/4 cup grated Swiss cheese

6 to 8 thin slices boiled ham

Paprika to taste

In a 10 1/2-inch sauté pan, melt 1/4 cup butter. Stir in lemon juice, water, and salt. Add endives. Cover and simmer 30 minutes until tender, adding more water if needed. Drain. In 1-quart saucepan, melt remaining 1/4 cup butter. Blend in flour and cayenne. Gradually stir in milk and bring to a boil, stirring. Reduce heat, add half of the grated cheese, and cook over low heat, stirring, until cheese is melted. Remove from heat.

Preheat oven to 450°F. Wrap each endive with a slice of ham, leaving ends exposed. Arrange in shallow baking dish and cover with sauce and remaining grated cheese and paprika. Bake for 15 minutes. ⌒

Pot Roast Madeira

YIELD: 10 SERVINGS

1 cup chopped onion

1 tablespoon finely shredded orange peel

1/2 cup orange juice

1/2 of 6-ounce can (1/3 cup) frozen orange juice concentrate, thawed

1/3 cup water

1 teaspoon salt

1 teaspoon sugar

1 teaspoon ground coriander

1/2 teaspoon pepper

1/4 to 1/2 teaspoon ground cloves

1/4 teaspoon ground cumin

1 (3 1/2-pound) beef chuck roast

1 tablespoon cooking oil

1 tablespoon butter

1/4 cup water

2 tablespoons cornstarch

1/4 cup Madeira wine

Orange slices, for garnish (optional)

• • •

In a blender or food processor, combine the onion, orange peel, orange juice concentrate, water, salt, sugar, coriander, pepper, cloves, and cumin. Cover and blend or process until nearly smooth.

Trim the fat from the meat. Place the meat in a large bowl or a shallow baking dish and pour the orange juice mixture over it. Cover and marinate in the refrigerator for 4 to 6 hours, turning the meat occasionally to distribute the marinade evenly. Drain the meat, reserving marinade. Pat the meat dry with paper towels.

(continued)

. . . continued

In a 4½-quart Dutch oven, heat the oil and butter over medium-high heat. Add the meat and brown well on all sides, about 4 minutes per side. Drain off the excess fat and discard.

Pour the reserved marinade over the meat and bring to a boil. Reduce the heat and simmer, covered, for 2 to 2½ hours, or until the meat is tender. Transfer the pot roast to a warm serving dish and cover to keep warm.

Stir together ¼ cup water and cornstarch and then stir into the cooking liquid. Add the Madeira. Cook, stirring constantly, until the sauce is thickened and bubbly. Cook and stir 2 minutes more. Serve the sauce over the meat. Garnish with orange slices, if desired. ᴧ

Bellflowers Pasta with White Clam Sauce

YIELD: 6 TO 8 SERVINGS

36 small hard-shell clams
   (at least)

$1/4$ cup olive oil

4 whole cloves garlic

$1/4$ teaspoon freshly ground
   black pepper

$1/4$ teaspoon oregano

3 tablespoons minced parsley

$1/4$ teaspoon basil

1 pound bellflowers pasta,
   cooked al dente and drained

Scrub the clams and rinse under cold running water until water runs clear. Heat the oil in a heavy saucepan. Brown the garlic cloves and then discard. Add the clams, pepper, oregano, parsley, and basil. Cover the pan and cook over low heat for 10 minutes. Let stand 5 minutes and then pour over bellflowers pasta.

Pasta and Zucchini

YIELD: 6 SERVINGS

2 quarts water

8 ounces large pasta shells

3 tablespoons butter

2 1/2 cups sliced zucchini

1/4 cup sliced green onions

2 cloves garlic, minced

1 tablespoon snipped fresh
   parsley

1/2 teaspoon Italian seasoning

1/4 cup grated Parmesan cheese

In a large kettle, bring the water to a boil. Gradually add the pasta and boil for 12 to 15 minutes, or until the pasta is tender but firm (al dente). Drain well.

Meanwhile, in a large skillet, melt the butter. Add the zucchini, green onion, garlic, and parsley. Cook and stir for about 10 minutes, or until the vegetables are tender. Remove from heat.

Add the cooked pasta to the zucchini mixture along with the Italian seasoning. Heat and toss for 2 to 3 minutes, or until heated through and well mixed. Remove from heat. Add half of the Parmesan cheese and toss. Sprinkle the remaining Parmesan cheese on top, and serve.

Menemsha-by-the-sea, Martha's Vineyard

Side Dishes

Aunt Ella's Macaroni and Cheese

YIELD: 6 SERVINGS

8 ounces elbow macaroni or
  assorted pasta, such as small
  shells, spirals, and wagon
  wheels

1 tablespoon butter, softened

1 egg, well beaten

1 teaspoon dry mustard

1/2 teaspoon salt

1/8 teaspoon ground nutmeg

1 tablespoon boiling water

1 cup milk

3 cups shredded sharp cheddar
  cheese

1/4 cup grated onion

Paprika to taste

Preheat oven to 350°F. Cook the macaroni in boiling water following the package directions until al dente (tender, but firm to the bite). Drain the macaroni and return to the saucepan. Stir in the butter and egg.

In a large bowl, combine the mustard, salt, and nutmeg with the tablespoon of boiling water. Stir in the milk, 2 1/2 cups of the cheese, onion, and macaroni. Pour the macaroni mixture into a lightly greased 1 1/2-quart casserole dish. Top with remaining cheese. Sprinkle with paprika. Bake for 1 hour, or until a well-browned top crust has formed. ∾

Gingered Carrots and Squash

YIELD: 6 SERVINGS

2 cups chicken broth

10 carrots, peeled and sliced

1 cup water

1 large onion, chopped

3 yellow (summer) squash, sliced

1/4 cup butter

1 teaspoon thyme

1 teaspoon ground ginger

1 teaspoon ground coriander

2 tablespoons honey

1/2 teaspoon salt

Bring broth to a boil in a large saucepan. Add carrots and water. Return to boil, cover, and reduce heat. Simmer 20 minutes, or just until tender but not mushy. Drain carrots, reserving liquid. Sauté onions and squash in butter over medium heat for 15 minutes, or just until onions are translucent, but not browned. Add carrots and remaining ingredients and cook 5 minutes more. Pour mixture into a food processor and puree. If too thick, add a little of the cooking liquid until the mixture is the consistency of mashed potatoes.

Honeyed Squash and Apples

YIELD: 6 SERVINGS

2 1/4 pounds butternut squash, peeled, seeded, and cut into 3/4-inch slices

1/4 cup butter

1/4 cup honey

1/4 cup orange juice

1/2 teaspoon ground cinnamon

1/4 teaspoon pumpkin pie spice

2 small, tart apples, peeled, cored, and sliced

Chopped walnuts (optional)

Preheat oven to 350°F. Place squash in an oiled 11 1/2 × 7 × 1 1/2-inch baking dish and set aside.

Combine butter, honey, orange juice, cinnamon, and pumpkin pie spice in a small saucepan. Bring to a boil over medium heat, stirring constantly. Pour 1/2 cup of mixture over squash. Toss apples with remaining mixture and set aside. Cover squash and bake 20 to 30 minutes. Uncover and add apple slices, in layers, alternating a layer of squash and a layer of apples. Bake, uncovered, for an additional 20 to 30 minutes, or until tender. Sprinkle with chopped walnuts. ∾

Onion Mashed Potatoes

YIELD: 4 SERVINGS

2 slices bacon

4 medium russet or baking
potatoes

$^{1}/_{2}$ teaspoon salt

$^{1}/_{8}$ teaspoon pepper

$^{1}/_{2}$ cup skim milk, heated

2 tablespoons chopped green
onions

2 ounces ($^{1}/_{2}$ cup) shredded
cheddar cheese

Cook bacon until crisp. Drain in paper towel. Crumble and set aside. Place potatoes in medium saucepan, adding enough water to cover. Bring to a boil. Reduce heat to medium low, cover loosely, and boil gently for 15 to 20 minutes, or until potatoes break apart easily when pierced with a fork. Drain well. Mash the potatoes until no lumps remain. Add salt, pepper, and milk and continue mashing until smooth. Spoon potatoes into serving dish. Top with onions, cheese, and bacon.

Orange Sherried Sweet Potatoes

YIELD: 8 SERVINGS

4 cups mashed cooked sweet
   potatoes

1/4 cup orange marmalade

2 tablespoons dry sherry

2 tablespoons butter, melted

1/2 teaspoon salt

1/3 cup finely chopped pecans

Preheat oven to 325°F. In large bowl, combine all ingredients except pecans, and blend well. Spoon into ungreased 1- to 1½-quart casserole or soufflé dish. Sprinkle with pecans.

Bake for 50 to 60 minutes, or until thoroughly heated. ∾

Summertime Squash

YIELD: 4 SERVINGS

2 small zucchini

2 small yellow squash

1 large red bell pepper

2 cloves garlic

2 teaspoons cornstarch

$1/4$ teaspoon salt

1 cup vegetable broth

1 tablespoon vegetable oil

1 teaspoon butter

Wash zucchini and yellow squash; pat dry with paper towels and cut off ends. Cut zucchini and yellow squash into diagonal slices, $1/4$-inch thick. Cut red bell pepper lengthwise in half. Remove stem and seeds. Rinse, dry, and cut into $1/4$-inch-thick strips. Finely chop garlic.

In a medium bowl, combine cornstarch and salt. Stir in vegetable broth until mixture is smooth; set aside. Heat large skillet over medium heat 1 minute or until hot. Drizzle vegetable oil into skillet. Add butter; swirl to coat bottom and heat 1 minute. Add zucchini and yellow squash; cook and stir 8 minutes or until crisp-tender. Stir in red bell pepper and garlic. Cook, stirring constantly, for about 1 minute. Stir reserved broth mixture until smooth and add to skillet. Cook and stir until sauce boils and thickens. Serve at once.

Twice-Baked Squash

YIELD: 6 SERVINGS

3 small butternut squash (about
   2 pounds), cut in half, and
   seeds and fibers discarded

$1/3$ cup nonfat sour cream

$1/2$ teaspoon salt

$1/4$ teaspoon nutmeg

6 tablespoons brown sugar

Preheat oven to 425°F. Place squash in ungreased 13 × 9-inch (3-quart) baking dish. Cover tightly with foil. Bake for 30 to 40 minutes, or until squash is tender. Cool 10 minutes. Reduce oven temperature to 375°F.

Scoop out squash, leaving $1/4$-inch thick shell, placing squash in medium bowl. Reserve shells. Add sour cream, salt, and nutmeg and mix until smooth. Fill each squash shell with squash mixture. Sprinkle each with 1 tablespoon brown sugar. Place filled shells in same baking dish and bake at 375°F for 15 to 20 minutes or until thoroughly heated. ∾

Veggie Stuffed Squash

YIELD: 2 SERVINGS

1 medium acorn squash (about 1½ pounds), halved and seeds removed

1 carrot, shredded

1 small zucchini, shredded

2 tablespoons finely chopped onion

2 tablespoons butter, melted

½ cup seasoned (Italian style) breadcrumbs

2 ounces (½ cup) shredded Parmesan cheese

1 egg, beaten

Dash of salt

Preheat oven to 375°F. Spray 12 × 8-inch (2-quart) baking dish with nonstick spray. Place squash cut sides down in sprayed baking dish. Bake for 40 minutes.

Meanwhile, in medium saucepan, combine carrot, zucchini, onion, and 1 tablespoon butter. Cook over medium heat for 3 to 5 minutes or until crisp-tender, stirring occasionally. Remove from heat. Add breadcrumbs, cheese, and egg, and mix well.

Remove squash from oven. Turn squash cut sides up and sprinkle with salt. Spoon vegetable mixture into squash halves. Top filled halves with remaining tablespoon butter. Return to oven; bake an additional 15 to 20 minutes until squash is tender and vegetable stuffing is set. ❧

Zucchini Special

YIELD: 8 SERVINGS

5 medium zucchini

10 mushrooms, medium size

1 large onion

2 tablespoons all-purpose flour

1 tablespoon fresh parsley

2 teaspoons baking powder

4 teaspoons fresh garlic

1 small can chopped green chiles
(4 ounces)

6 large eggs, beaten

3 cups shredded cheddar cheese

4 tablespoons butter, melted

1 cup crushed corn flakes

Preheat the oven to 350°F, lightly coat the bottom and sides of a 13 × 9-inch baking dish with canola oil. Slice the zucchini into $1/8$-inch slices. Slice the mushrooms and mince the onion.

Combine flour, parsley, baking powder, and garlic in a large bowl and mix well. Stir in the green chiles and add the beaten eggs.

Layer half the zucchini, mushrooms, onion, cheddar, egg mixture, butter, and corn flakes (should be sprinkled on top). Bake Zucchini Special until set, about 30 to 35 minutes.

Norton's Peir, Edgartown

Breads and Muffins

Apple Crumble Coffee Cake

Topping:

2 tablespoons firm butter

1/4 cup flour

1/4 cup light brown sugar

1/2 teaspoon ground cinnamon

1/4 cup old fashioned rolled oats

Apples:

1 3/4 cups flour

1 cup light brown sugar, packed

3/4 cup old-fashioned rolled oats

3 teaspoons baking powder

1/2 teaspoon baking soda

1 teaspoon ground cinnamon

1/2 teaspoon salt

1/2 teaspoon ground nutmeg

1/2 cup butter, softened

1 large egg

1 cup buttermilk

3 cups peeled, chopped apples

• • •

Prepare topping by cutting butter into flour, brown sugar, and cinnamon in a medium bowl, until crumbly. Add oats and mix well. Set aside.

Preheat oven to 350°F. To prepare apples, combine all dry ingredients, and mix well. Add butter, egg, and buttermilk and beat with electric mixer on medium speed for 2 minutes, scraping sides of bowl as necessary. Stir in apples and mix well. Pour batter into oiled casserole and spread evenly. Sprinkle topping mixture over batter. Bake for 50 to 55 minutes, or until golden brown and toothpick inserted into middle comes out clean. Cool on a wire rack. Serve warm. May be served with vanilla ice cream or whipped cream. ∾

Banana-Stuffed French Toast

YIELD: 2 SERVINGS

2 eggs

1/3 cup milk

1/4 teaspoon cinnamon

1/2 teaspoon vanilla extract

4 bread slices, 1 inch thick

1 medium banana, thinly sliced

8 teaspoons coconut

1 tablespoon butter

Heat skillet to medium-high heat or griddle to 375°F. In shallow pan, combine eggs, milk, cinnamon, and vanilla, and beat well. Split each bread slice in half, horizontally, leaving 1 edge attached. Pull back top layer of each bread slice and spread 1 tablespoon of the egg mixture on bottom layer. Place 1/4 of banana slices and 2 teaspoons of coconut on the egg mixture on each slice.

Melt butter in skillet. Dip each stuffed bread slice into egg mixture to coat both sides. Cook 4 minutes on each side or until golden brown. Serve with additional banana slices, toasted coconut, and maple syrup.

Best of the Cape Gingerbread

YIELD: 6 TO 8 SERVINGS

1 1/2 cups self-rising flour

2 teaspoons ground ginger

1 teaspoon ground allspice

1/2 teaspoon salt

1 teaspoon baking soda

1/2 cup unsalted butter

1/2 cup dark brown sugar, soft

3 eggs, beaten

1 cup molasses

Preheat oven to 325°F. Sift flour, ginger, allspice, salt, and baking soda into a bowl. In another bowl, cream the butter and brown sugar until very soft. Add the beaten eggs, mixing well. Then add molasses and mix. Gently fold in the sifted dry ingredients.

Pour the batter into an oiled and lined 8-inch square, deep baking pan and bake for 50 to 60 minutes, or until the top springs back when pressed gently.

Cool in the pan. Remove and store for a few days in an airtight tin before serving. Serve warm with whipped cream.

Berry Citrus Muffins

YIELD: 12 MUFFINS

2 cups flour

1/2 cup sugar

3 teaspoons baking powder

1 teaspoon grated lemon or
  orange peel

1/2 teaspoon salt

1/2 cup orange juice

1/2 cup butter, melted

1 egg

3/4 cup fresh or frozen
  blueberries (do not thaw)

3/4 cup fresh or frozen
  raspberries (do not thaw)

Preheat oven to 400°F. Line 12 muffin cups with paper baking cups or grease bottoms only. In large bowl, combine flour, sugar, baking powder, lemon peel, and salt. In small bowl, combine juice, butter, and egg and blend well. Add to dry ingredients and stir just until dry ingredients are moistened. (Batter will be very thick.) Gently stir in berries. Fill muffin cups 3/4 full.

Bake for 18 to 25 minutes or until light golden brown and until toothpick inserted in center comes out clean. Cool 1 minute. Remove from muffin cups.

Blueberry Muffins

⅓ cup butter

⅔ to 1 cup sugar, depending on
   sweetness of berries

1 egg

1 cup milk

2 cups flour

½ to 1 teaspoon salt

1 teaspoon baking powder

1 heaping cup blueberries

Preheat oven to 350°F. Line muffin cups with paper baking cups or grease bottoms only. Cream butter and sugar. Add egg and beat well. Add milk alternately with flour, salt, and baking powder. Add blueberries last. Fill buttered muffin tins ⅔ full and bake for 20 to 30 minutes, depending on size of muffin tins. ∾

Boston Brown Bread

YIELD: 1 LOAF

2 cups whole wheat flour

1 cup flour

2 teaspoons baking soda

1 teaspoon salt

2/3 cup firmly packed brown
  sugar

1/4 cup unsulphured molasses

2 cups buttermilk

1 cup raisins

Preheat oven to 350°F. Oil a 9 × 5-inch loaf pan and dust with flour, knocking out excess flour. In a large bowl, mix together dry ingredients. Stir in remaining ingredients until just combined. Do not overmix. Pour batter into prepared pan and bake in middle of the oven until a toothpick inserted in the middle comes out clean and dry, about 1 hour. Cool bread in pan on a rack for 5 minutes. Turn bread out onto rack, and cool completely before slicing. ᗡ

Cape Cod Spicy Pumpkin Bread

YIELD: 1 LOAF

1^1/$_2$ cups sugar

1^2/$_3$ cups flour

1 teaspoon baking soda

^{1}/$_4$ teaspoon baking powder

^{1}/$_2$ teaspoon cinnamon

^{1}/$_4$ teaspoon ground nutmeg

^{1}/$_4$ teaspoon ground ginger

^{1}/$_4$ teaspoon ground cloves

^{1}/$_4$ teaspoon ground allspice

1 cup pumpkin

^{1}/$_2$ cup vegetable oil

^{1}/$_2$ cup water

2 eggs, well beaten

^{1}/$_2$ cup raisins

^{1}/$_2$ cup chopped walnuts

Preheat oven to 350°F. Combine dry ingredients. Add all other ingredients and mix well. Pour into greased and floured loaf pan. Bake for 1 hour.

Interior of casino, Falmouth Heights

Cheddar Olive Bread

YIELD: 12

2 1/2 cups all-purpose flour

2 tablespoons sugar

2 teaspoons baking powder

1 teaspoon dry mustard

1/2 teaspoon baking soda

1/2 teaspoon salt

1/4 teaspoon cayenne pepper

4 tablespoons butter

4 ounces cheddar cheese

1 cup buttermilk

1 teaspoon Worcestershire sauce

1 large egg

1 cup pimiento-stuffed green olives, chopped

3/4 cup corn kernels

Preheat the oven to 375°F. Coat bottom and sides of a 9 × 5-inch loaf pan lightly with vegetable oil. Sift the flour, sugar, baking powder, dry mustard, baking soda, salt, and cayenne pepper into a medium bowl and mix well. Cut in butter with a pastry blender until mixture is crumbly. Add cheddar to the flour mixture and mix well.

Make a well in the center of flour mixture. Whisk buttermilk, Worcestershire sauce, and egg in a small bowl until blended. Pour into the well, stirring just until moistened. Next, stir in olives and corn.

Pour batter into prepared loaf pan. Bake until a toothpick inserted in center comes out clean, about 45 minutes. Cool bread in pan for 5 to 10 minutes. Remove to a wire rack to cool completely. Slice and serve. Store leftovers in refrigerator. ❧

Cranberry Banana Nut Scones

YIELD: 8 SCONES

2 $^1/_2$ cups flour

$^1/_2$ cup brown sugar

2 teaspoons baking powder

1 $^1/_2$ teaspoons nutmeg

1 teaspoon salt

$^1/_2$ cup butter, softened

2 cups fresh or frozen
  cranberries, chopped

3 ripe bananas, mashed

$^1/_2$ cup chopped walnuts

1 egg

Preheat oven to 350°F. Combine dry ingredients in medium mixing bowl. Using pastry blender or fork, work butter into dry ingredients until butter is the size of small peas.

Combine cranberries, banana, walnuts, and egg in a medium mixing bowl. Add to dry ingredients, mixing thoroughly.

Spread batter into a 10-inch circle on an ungreased cookie sheet. Cut into 8 wedges. Bake for 25 minutes or until golden brown. Remove scones from oven and re-cut wedges. Serve warm. ∾

Cranberry Coffee Cake

YIELD: 8 SERVINGS

Cake:

3 tablespoons butter, melted

1/2 cup light brown sugar

1 1/2 cups whole fresh cranberries

3 tablespoons butter

1/2 cup white sugar

1 egg, well beaten

1 1/2 cups flour

2 teaspoons baking powder

1/2 teaspoon salt

1/2 cup milk

Sauce:

1/2 cup butter

1 cup light brown sugar

4 tablespoons cream

1 teaspoon vanilla extract

Preheat oven to 400°F. To prepare cake, mix melted butter and brown sugar together, and press into the bottom of a 9-inch square cake pan. Pour cranberries over this mixture. Cream butter and sugar until light and fluffy. Add egg and mix well. Sift flour, baking powder, and salt together and add alternately with milk until all ingredients are thoroughly blended. Pour batter over cranberries in bottom of cake pan. Bake for 25 minutes or until done.

To prepare sauce, melt butter and sugar together in a saucepan over low to medium heat, stirring constantly. Add cream and vanilla, stir until blended, and remove from heat. Pour sauce over cake and serve warm. ∾

Gingerbread Bars

YIELD: 36 BARS

1/2 cup sugar

1/2 cup oil

1/2 cup molasses

1 egg

1 1/2 cups flour

3/4 teaspoon baking soda

1/2 teaspoon cinnamon

1/2 teaspoon salt

1/4 teaspoon nutmeg

1/4 teaspoon cloves

1/4 cup boiling water

1/2 cup granola

1/2 cup raisins

Preheat oven to 350°F. In large bowl, beat sugar, oil, and molasses until well blended. Add egg and blend well. Add flour, baking soda, cinnamon, salt, nutmeg, and cloves and mix well. Add boiling water, blending well. Stir in granola and raisins. Spread in oiled 13 x 9-inch pan.

Bake for 20 to 30 minutes or until toothpick inserted in center comes out clean. Cool completely. Cut into bars. ❧

Golden Harvest Muffins

YIELD: 36 MUFFINS

2 cups flour

2 cups whole wheat flour

2 cups sugar

4 teaspoons baking soda

4 teaspoons cinnamon

1 teaspoon salt

1/2 teaspoon cloves

1 cup shredded carrots

4 cups (5 medium) peeled,
   shredded apples

1 cup coconut

1 cup raisins

1 cup chopped walnuts or
   pecans

1 1/2 cups vegetable oil

1/2 cup milk

4 teaspoons vanilla extract

3 eggs, beaten

Preheat oven to 350°F. Line 36 muffin cups with paper baking cups or grease bottoms only. In 4-quart bowl, combine all-purpose flour, whole wheat flour, sugar, baking soda, cinnamon, salt, and cloves. Add carrots, apples, coconut, raisins, and chopped nuts and mix well. Add oil, milk, vanilla, and eggs and stir just until moistened. Fill lined or greased muffin cups 3/4 full.

Bake for 20 to 25 minutes or until toothpick inserted in center comes out clean. Immediately remove from pans. ∾

Hearty Oatmeal Cranberry Muffins

YIELD: 6 MUFFINS

1 cup biscuit mix

2 cups oatmeal

1/2 cup brown sugar

2 teaspoons cinnamon

1 egg

1/4 cup oil

1/2 cup milk

1/2 cup whole berry cranberry
   sauce

Preheat oven to 375°F. Combine biscuit mix, oatmeal, brown sugar, and cinnamon in a medium mixing bowl. Combine egg, oil, and milk in a separate mixing bowl. Add to dry ingredients, mixing just until moist.

Grease a 6-cup muffin tin. Fill each muffin cup 1/3 full with batter. Spoon about 1/2 tablespoon cranberry sauce into the center of each cup. Top with enough batter to cover sauce.

Bake for 22 minutes or until golden brown. Cool slightly and remove from pan. ∾

Placing cranberries in trays, Cape Cod

Lemon Bread

YIELD: 1 LOAF

Bread:

6 tablespoons butter, softened

1 cup sugar

2 eggs

1^1/$_2$ cups presifted flour

1 teaspoon salt

1 teaspoon baking powder

Grated rind of 1 lemon

^{1}/$_2$ cup milk

Chopped nuts (optional)

Topping:

^{1}/$_3$ cup sugar

Juice of 1 lemon

Preheat oven to 325°F. Prepare the bread by mixing the butter, sugar, and eggs in a food processor or blender. Add the flour, salt, and baking powder. Blend milk alternately with flour mixture into the batter. Mix in the grated lemon rind and nuts (optional). Bake in an 8 × 5-inch loaf pan for 45 to 60 minutes. Remove from oven and let cool for 10 minutes.

Prepare the topping by mixing the sugar and lemon juice. Place warm loaf on wax paper and slowly drizzle topping mixture on top of hot loaf. Cool. Store in refrigerator.

Mother's Old-Fashioned Gingerbread

YIELD: 9 SERVINGS

Bread:

1³/4 cups flour

1 teaspoon ginger

¹/2 teaspoon salt

1 teaspoon baking soda

1 cup hot water

¹/3 cup shortening melted in
   water

³/4 cup molasses

Fruit Compote:

2 cups fresh cranberries

3 cups pineapple chunks, cut in
   half

1 cup brown sugar

1 teaspoon cinnamon

¹/4 teaspoon nutmeg

Whipped cream

Preheat oven to 350°F. Sift together flour, ginger, salt, and baking soda. Add water, melted shortening, and molasses. Mix well. Pour into greased baking pan. Bake for 30 minutes. Remove from oven and let cool completely.

While gingerbread is cooling, combine all compote ingredients except whipped cream in a medium saucepan. Bring mixture to a boil and cook just until cranberries begin to pop, stirring frequently. Cool slightly. Spoon warm compote over each serving of gingerbread. Top with whipped cream. ❧

New England Spoonbread

YIELD: 1 LOAF

1½ cups water

1½ cups half-and-half (milk and cream)

1 cup coarse stone-ground yellow cornmeal

¼ cup chopped fresh flat parsley

1 teaspoon salt

2 whole tomatoes, seeded and chopped (about 2 cups)

¼ cup butter, softened

4 large eggs, separated

2 tablespoons minced seeded jalapeño peppers (optional)

Preheat oven to 350°F. In a large saucepan, bring water to a boil. Reduce heat to low. In a medium bowl, combine half-and-half, cornmeal, parsley, salt, and tomato. Whisk mixture into hot water. Cook, stirring, until mixture thickens and bubbles, about 5 minutes. Stir in butter.

In a medium bowl, beat egg yolks. Whisk the hot cornmeal mixture into the egg yolks, a little at a time, stirring constantly. Turn mixture back into the saucepan, stirring rapidly to prevent lumping. Cook over low heat, stirring constantly, until mixture bubbles again, about 2 minutes. Remove from heat.

In a large bowl, beat egg whites until stiff peaks form. Using a rubber spatula, fold egg whites into hot cornmeal mixture until just blended. Pour mixture into an oiled medium casserole dish. Bake until golden brown and a knife inserted in the center comes out clean, about 40 minutes. ❧

Onion Chive Muffins

YIELD: 12 MUFFINS

3/4 cup chopped onions

1 teaspoon vegetable oil

1 1/2 cups flour

1/4 cup chopped fresh chives

2 tablespoons sugar

2 teaspoons baking powder

1/2 teaspoon salt

1/4 teaspoon baking soda

1 cup buttermilk

1/4 cup vegetable oil

1 egg, slightly beaten

Preheat oven to 375°F. Grease bottoms of 12 muffin cups or line with paper baking cups. In small skillet, over medium heat, cook and stir onions in 1 teaspoon of oil until crisp-tender; set aside.

In large bowl, combine flour, chives, sugar, baking powder, salt, and baking soda. In small bowl, combine cooked onions, buttermilk, 1/4 cup oil, and egg and mix well. Add to dry ingredients, stirring just until dry ingredients are moistened. Fill greased muffin cups about 3/4 full.

Bake for 12 to 14 minutes, or until toothpick inserted in center comes out clean. Immediately remove from pans. ∾

Oven-Puffed Pancake with Fruit Topping

YIELD: 2 TO 4 SERVINGS

Pancake:

1/2 cup flour

2 tablespoons sugar

1/4 teaspoon salt

1/2 cup milk

2 eggs

2 tablespoons butter

Topping:

1/2 cup sugar

1 tablespoon cornstarch

1/2 cup orange juice

2 tablespoons orange-flavored
  liqueur or orange juice

3 cups sliced fruits and/or
  berries

Preheat oven to 425°F. In medium bowl, combine all pancake ingredients except butter. Beat with wire whisk until smooth. Place butter in 9-inch pie pan; melt in oven just until butter sizzles, 2 to 4 minutes. Remove pan from oven, tilting to coat bottom with melted butter. Immediately pour batter into hot pan. Bake for 14 to 18 minutes, or until puffed and golden brown. (Some butter may rise to surface of pancake during cooking.)

Meanwhile, in small saucepan, combine 1/2 cup sugar and cornstarch and mix well. Stir in orange juice and liqueur. Cook and stir over medium heat 5 to 7 minutes, or until sugar dissolves and mixture thickens. Remove pancake from oven. Immediately arrange peaches and strawberries over pancake and drizzle with orange sauce. Serve immediately. ～

Pumpkin Maple Corn Muffins

YIELD: 12 MUFFINS

1 cup yellow cornmeal

1 cup flour

$1/2$ teaspoon salt

2 teaspoons baking powder

1 teaspoon baking soda

6 tablespoons unsalted butter

$1/2$ cup firmly packed brown
   sugar

$1/2$ cup canned pumpkin (or
   baked sweet potato, mashed)

2 eggs, lightly beaten

$1/2$ cup milk

$1/2$ cup pure maple syrup

Preheat oven to 350°F. In a large bowl, combine cornmeal, flour, salt, baking powder, and soda. In another bowl, cream together the butter and brown sugar. Add the pumpkin and eggs. Then mix in the milk and maple syrup, beating well. Make a well in the center of the dry ingredients and pour the pumpkin mixture in, stirring until just combined. Fill oiled muffin tins $3/4$ full with batter. Bake for 25 minutes. ～

Pumpkin Seed Muffins

YIELD: 12 MUFFINS

1³/4 cups flour

1/2 cup sugar

1/4 cup toasted pumpkin seeds, chopped

3 teaspoons baking powder

1 teaspoon cinnamon

1/2 teaspoon salt

3/4 cup milk

1/2 cup pumpkin puree

1/3 cup oil

1 egg, well beaten

Preheat oven to 400°F. Line with paper cups or grease 12 muffin cups. In large bowl, combine flour, sugar, pumpkin seeds, baking powder, cinnamon, and salt, and mix well. In small bowl, combine remaining ingredients. Add to dry ingredients and stir just until moistened. (Batter will be lumpy.) Divide batter evenly among muffin cups. Bake for 20 to 25 minutes, or until tops spring back when lightly touched. Immediately remove from pan. Serve warm. ◡

Zucchini Bread

3 eggs

1 cup vegetable oil

2 1/2 cups sugar

2 cups grated zucchini with skin
(best with firm, fresh, and very
large zucchini)

3 cups flour

1 teaspoon baking powder

1 teaspoon baking soda

1 teaspoon salt

2 teaspoons cinnamon

1/2 cup chopped walnuts

1/2 cup raisins

Preheat oven to 350°F. Use 2 greased and floured 8 × 5-inch loaf pans. Beat eggs. Add oil, sugar, and zucchini, and mix well by hand. Add flour and all other dry ingredients, mixing well. Add chopped nuts and raisins last, and mix well. Bake for 1 hour 20 minutes. ◦

Idle Hour Theatre, Hyannis

Cookies

Carrot Raisin Bran Cookies

YIELD: 5½ DOZEN COOKIES

1 cup firmly packed brown sugar

1 cup softened butter

1 cup (2 medium) shredded carrots

1 teaspoon vanilla extract

1 egg

1½ cups flour

1 teaspoon cinnamon

½ teaspoon baking soda

2½ cups bran flakes cereal with raisins

Preheat oven to 375°F. In large bowl, beat brown sugar and butter until light and fluffy. Add carrots, vanilla, and egg, blending well. Stir in flour, cinnamon, and baking soda and mix well. Stir in cereal. Drop dough by rounded teaspoonfuls 2 inches apart onto ungreased baking sheets.

Bake for 9 to 14 minutes or until light golden brown. Cool 1 minute and remove from baking sheets. ∽

Cranberry and Orange Pinwheels

YIELD: 3 DOZEN COOKIES

Filling:

1 tablespoon cornstarch

3/4 cup whole berry cranberry
sauce

1/2 cup orange marmalade

Cookies:

3/4 cup firmly packed brown
sugar

1/2 cup butter, softened

1 egg

1 3/4 cups flour

1 teaspoon baking powder

1 teaspoon grated orange peel

1/4 teaspoon salt

1/4 teaspoon allspice

In small saucepan, combine all filling ingredients. Bring to a boil over medium heat, stirring constantly. Refrigerate until thoroughly chilled.

In large bowl, beat brown sugar, butter, and egg until light and fluffy. Stir in flour, baking powder, orange peel, salt, and allspice and mix well. Cover with plastic wrap. Refrigerate for 1 hour for easier handling.

On lightly floured surface, roll dough into 16 × 8-inch rectangle. Spoon and spread cooled filling evenly over dough to within 1/2 inch of edges. Starting with 16-inch side, roll up jelly-roll fashion and cut in half to form two 8-inch rolls. Wrap tightly in plastic wrap or waxed paper and freeze at least 2 hours.

Preheat oven to 375°F. Generously grease cookie sheets. Using sharp knife, cut dough into 1/2-inch thick slices. Place 2 inches apart on greased cookie sheets. Bake for 9 to 13 minutes, or until light golden brown. Immediately remove from cookie sheets. ∾

Cranberry Orange Cookies

YIELD: 3 1/2 DOZEN COOKIES

1/2 cup sugar

1/2 cup powdered sugar

1/2 cup butter

1/2 cup vegetable oil

2 teaspoons grated orange rind

1 teaspoon vanilla extract

1 egg

2 cups flour

1/2 teaspoon baking soda

1/2 teaspoon cream of tartar

1/4 teaspoon salt

1/2 cup chopped cranberries

Powdered sugar (optional)

Preheat oven to 350°F. In large bowl, beat sugar, powdered sugar, butter, and oil until well blended. Add orange rind, vanilla, and egg, and blend well. Stir in flour, baking soda, cream of tartar, and salt, and mix well. Stir in cranberries.

Drop dough by rounded teaspoonfuls 2 inches apart onto ungreased cookie sheets. Bake for 10 to 15 minutes, or until bottoms are light golden brown. Cool 1 minute and remove from cookie sheets. Cool completely. Sprinkle with powdered sugar.

Fresh Orange Cookies

YIELD: 6 DOZEN COOKIES

Cookies:

1¹/₂ cups sugar

1 cup butter, softened

1 cup dairy sour cream

2 eggs

4 cups flour

1 teaspoon baking powder

1 teaspoon baking soda

¹/₂ teaspoon salt

²/₃ cup orange juice

3 tablespoons grated orange peel

Frosting:

¹/₄ cup butter, melted

2 cups powdered sugar

1 tablespoon grated orange peel

2 to 3 tablespoons orange juice

Preheat oven to 375°F. In large bowl, beat sugar and 1 cup butter until light and fluffy. Add sour cream and eggs and blend well. Stir in flour and remaining cookie ingredients, mixing well. Drop dough by rounded teaspoonfuls onto ungreased cookie sheets. Bake for 8 to 11 minutes, or until edges are light golden brown. Immediately remove from cookie sheets.

In small bowl, combine all frosting ingredients, adding enough orange juice for desired spreading consistency. Frost warm cookies.

Lemon Butter Cookies

YIELD: 3 1/2 DOZEN COOKIES

1/2 cup sugar

1/2 cup powdered sugar

3/4 cup butter, softened

1/4 cup oil

1 tablespoon grated lemon peel

1 tablespoon lemon juice

1 egg

2 1/2 cups flour

1/2 teaspoon cream of tartar

1/2 teaspoon baking soda

1/4 teaspoon salt

Yellow decorator sugar

In large bowl, beat sugar, powdered sugar, butter, and oil until light and fluffy. Add lemon peel, lemon juice, and egg and blend well. Stir in flour, cream of tartar, baking soda, and salt, mixing well. Cover with plastic wrap and refrigerate 1 hour for easier handling.

Preheat oven to 350°F. Shape dough into 1-inch balls and roll in sugar. Place 2 inches apart on ungreased cookie sheets. Bake for 7 to 12 minutes or until set. Immediately remove from cookie sheets. ∽

Oat and Banana Cookies

YIELD: 4 DOZEN COOKIES

1¹/₂ cups flour

1 cup sugar

1 teaspoon baking powder

1 teaspoon ground cinnamon

¹/₂ teaspoon ground nutmeg

¹/₂ teaspoon salt

¹/₂ teaspoon baking soda

²/₃ cup shortening

2 eggs

1 cup mashed ripe bananas
  (2 or 3)

1¹/₂ cups rolled oats

Preheat oven to 375°F. In a large mixing bowl, stir together the flour, sugar, baking powder, cinnamon, nutmeg, salt, and baking soda. Add the shortening, eggs, and half of the mashed bananas. Beat about 2 minutes or until creamy with an electric mixer on low speed. Add the remaining mashed bananas and oats. Drop by teaspoonfuls onto greased cookie sheets.

Bake for about 10 minutes, or until lightly browned. Using a spatula, transfer the cookies from the cookie sheets to a wire rack to cool.

Sugar Drop Cookies

YIELD: 1½ TO 2 DOZEN COOKIES

2 cups all-purpose flour, sifted

2 teaspoons baking powder

½ teaspoon salt

2 large eggs

¾ cup sugar

⅔ cup vegetable oil

2 teaspoons vanilla extract

1 teaspoon grated lemon zest

2 tablespoons extra sugar for topping

Sift flour, baking powder, and salt into a medium bowl and mix well. Whisk eggs in a large bowl until blended. Add sugar, oil, vanilla extract, and lemon zest and mix well. Stir the dry ingredients into the egg mixture until blended. Chill, covered with plastic wrap, for 30 minutes or longer. Now, preheat the oven to 400°F.

Drop the cookie dough by rounded teaspoonfuls 2 inches apart onto ungreased baking sheets. Mist the bottom of a 3-inch flat-bottom glass with water and dip glass in additional sugar. Press the top of each cookie lightly with the glass to flatten, misting glass with water and dipping in sugar before pressing each cookie.

Bake cookies until lightly browned, approximately 8 minutes. Cool on baking sheets for 2 minutes. Remove to wire racks to cool completely. Store in airtight containers or freeze for future use. ❧

Main Street, Chatham

Desserts

American Apple Pie

YIELD: 8 SERVINGS

2 tablespoons lemon juice

1 tablespoon cornstarch

1/3 cup packed light brown sugar

1/3 cup sugar

1 tablespoon butter, melted

1 teaspoon ground cinnamon

1 teaspoon ground nutmeg

1/4 teaspoon salt

6 cups peeled and sliced cooking
   apples

Pastry for 9-inch double crust
   pie

1 egg yolk, beaten with
   1 teaspoon water

Sugar to taste

In a small bowl, stir the lemon juice and cornstarch until well blended. In a large bowl, combine the brown sugar, sugar, butter, cinnamon, nutmeg, salt, and the cornstarch mixture. Add the apple slices and toss to coat the slices completely. Let the mixture stand for 10 minutes.

Preheat the oven to 450°F. Fill the pastry-lined pie plate with the apple mixture. Moisten the edges of pastry with a little water. Put on the top crust and flute the edge. Cut several vents in the top crust and brush the whole top crust with the egg yolk mixture. Lightly sprinkle with sugar.

Bake the pie at 450°F for 15 minutes, then lower to 350°F for 30 minutes, or until crust is golden brown. If necessary, cover the edges of the crust with foil to prevent over-browning. ∿

Apple Streusel Pie

YIELD: 8 TO 10 SERVINGS

Filling:

1 cup sugar

3 1/2 tablespoons flour

1/2 teaspoon cinnamon

1/2 teaspoon grated lemon peel
   (colored part only)

8 cups sliced apples

2 tablespoons butter

1 tablespoon lemon juice

Streusel Topping:

1/4 cup Grape Nuts cereal

1/3 cup white sugar

1/4 cup brown sugar

Pinch of salt

1 stick butter

1 teaspoon ground nutmeg

Preheat oven to 350°F. To prepare filling, mix sugar, flour, cinnamon, and lemon peel. Add apple slices and toss well to coat with flour mixture. Spread filling in 10-inch pie plate and dot with butter. Sprinkle lemon juice over filling.

Place on baking sheet and bake at 350°F for 20 minutes. Mix streusel topping to a chunky consistency while pie is baking. Remove hot pie and spread streusel topping evenly over pie. Return to oven and continue baking until golden brown, about 40 more minutes. ∾

Apricot Almond Cheesecake

Y I E L D : 1 6 S E R V I N G S

Crust:

1¹/₂ cups graham cracker crumbs

¹/₂ cup slivered almonds,
    coarsely ground

2 tablespoons brown sugar

¹/₃ cup butter, melted

*I*n medium bowl, combine all crust ingredients and mix well. Press mixture into bottom and 2 inches up the sides of 9-inch springform pan. Set aside.

(continued)

. . . continued

Filling:

4 ounces (³/₄ cup) dried apricots

¹/₂ cup water

1¹/₂ cups sugar

1 cup sugar

2 (8-ounce) packages cream
   cheese

1 (8-ounce) container dairy sour
   cream

1 teaspoon almond extract

3 eggs

In medium saucepan, prepare the filling by combining the apricots and the water. Cook, covered, over low heat for 15 minutes, or until apricots are tender. Stir in ¹/₂ cup sugar. Puree in blender or food processor with metal blade. Blend until mixture is smooth. Set aside to cool.

Preheat oven to 350°F. In large bowl, mix 1 cup sugar, cream cheese, sour cream, and almond extract. Add eggs 1 at a time, beating well until smooth and creamy. Blend 1 cup cream cheese mixture with apricot puree. Pour remaining cream cheese mixture into pan. Carefully drop spoonfuls of apricot mixture randomly over cream cheese filling. Pull knife through batter in wide curves; turn pan and repeat for swirl effect.

Bake 60 to 70 minutes until center is set. (To minimize cracking, place shallow pan half full of hot water on lower oven rack during baking.) Cool to room temperature. Carefully remove sides of pan. Cover and refrigerate at least 24 hours before serving. ∿

Baked Indian Pudding

4 cups milk

3 tablespoons cornmeal

1/2 cup sugar

1/2 teaspoon salt

1 teaspoon cinnamon

1/2 cup seedless raisins

1/2 cup molasses

2 eggs, beaten

Preheat oven to 300°F. In a double boiler, scald 2 cups milk. Slowly add cornmeal, stirring well. Combine and add sugar, salt, cinnamon, raisins, and molasses. Stir hot mixture into the beaten eggs and pour into greased uncovered casserole. Bake for 1 hour. Pour remaining 2 cups milk over top, and continue to bake for 1 hour without stirring. Serve hot with cream, ice cream, or maple syrup toppings. ∾

Banana Cake

1/2 cup butter

1 1/2 cups sugar

3 medium ripe bananas

1 cup chopped nuts

3 egg yolks

1/2 teaspoon baking soda

2 1/2 cups flour

1/2 teaspoon salt

1 teaspoon baking powder

3 tablespoons sour milk

6 tablespoons dark rum

Whites of eggs, beaten stiff

Preheat oven to 350°F. Cream butter and sugar. Add banana and nuts. Add egg yolks and other dry ingredients with milk. Add rum and egg whites. Bake for 1 hour.

Banana Cake (2)

1 1/4 cups sifted cake flour

3/4 teaspoon baking soda

1/2 teaspoon salt

1/2 cup butter, softened

1 cup sugar

2 eggs

3 medium ripe bananas

Preheat oven to 350°F. Sift together flour, baking soda, and salt. Using an electric mixer, cream butter and sugar, and continue beating until light and fluffy. Add eggs, one at a time, beating after each addition. Blend in mashed bananas. Add dry ingredients to banana mixture and mix well. Turn into greased and floured 9-inch square pan.

Bake for 35 minutes, or until toothpick inserted in the center comes out clean. Cool on wire rack. If desired, sift confectioners' sugar over cake or top with whipped cream. ∼

Entrance to Wychmere Harbor, Harwichport

Berry Cobbler

2 1/2 cups fresh raspberries

2 1/2 cups fresh blueberries

2 tablespoons cornstarch

1/2 cup sugar

1 cup all-purpose flour

1 1/2 teaspoons baking powder

1/4 teaspoon salt

1/3 cup butter

1/3 cup milk

2 tablespoons apple juice

1/4 teaspoon ground nutmeg

Preheat oven to 375°F. Mix raspberries, blueberries, and cornstarch in a bowl; toss lightly to coat berries. Add the sugar and mix well.

Spoon into 8-inch square baking dish. Combine flour, baking powder, and salt in a bowl; set aside. Melt butter and combine with milk and apple juice in a bowl; mix well. Stir milk mixture into flour mixture until dry ingredients are moistened. Evenly drop 6 heaping tablespoonfuls of dough over berries in baking dish, and sprinkle the ground nutmeg on top.

Bake 25 minutes, or until topping is golden and fruit is bubbly. Cool on a wire rack. Serve warm with whipped cream or vanilla ice cream on top.

Blueberry Grunt

YIELD: 6 TO 8 SERVINGS

2 cups fresh blueberries

1 cup water

1 cup plus 2 tablespoons sugar

1/4 teaspoon cinnamon

1 cup flour

1 1/4 teaspoons baking powder

1/4 teaspoon salt

1 egg, well beaten

1/4 cup milk

Cream (optional)

Wash and pick over blueberries. Put water in large, heavy skillet; add 1 cup sugar, and bring to a boil. Reduce heat, add berries and cinnamon, and let simmer while preparing the rest.

Sift dry ingredients into mixing bowl. Combine egg and milk and add to dry ingredients, including remaining 2 tablespoons sugar. Stir just enough to moisten. Drop dough by large spoonfuls on the boiling berries. Allow space between drops for dumplings to expand. Cook, uncovered, for 10 minutes. Cover skillet and cook 10 minutes longer. Serve warm with cream or whipped cream. ❧

Boston Cream Pie

YIELD: 8 SERVINGS

Cake:

1/2 cup butter or margarine

2 1/2 cups sifted cake flour

3 teaspoons baking powder

1/2 teaspoon salt

1 1/2 cups granulated sugar

3/4 cup plus 2 tablespoons milk

1 teaspoon vanilla extract

2 eggs

Cream filling

Confectioners' sugar

Preheat oven to 375°F. Stir butter just to soften. Sift in flour, baking powder, salt, and granulated sugar. Add 3/4 cup milk and the vanilla. Mix until dry ingredients are dampened. Then beat for 3 minutes at low speed of electric mixer or 300 vigorous strokes by hand. Add eggs and remaining milk. Beat for 1 minute longer or 150 strokes by hand.

Pour into 2 layer cake pans (9 inches) lined on the bottom with parchment paper. Bake for 20 to 25 minutes.

(continued)

. . . continued

Cream Filling:

$1/2$ cup sugar

$2^1/2$ tablespoons cornstarch

$1/8$ teaspoon salt

$1^1/2$ cups milk

2 egg yolks, beaten

1 teaspoon vanilla extract

While baking, prepare the cream filling. In heavy saucepan, mix sugar, cornstarch, and salt. Add $1/2$ cup milk and stir until smooth. Add remaining milk and cook over low heat, stirring constantly, until smooth and thickened. Stir mixture into egg yolks. Put back in saucepan and cook for 2 minutes longer, stirring constantly. Cool and add vanilla.

Turn baked cakes out on cake racks and peel off paper. Cool and put together with cream filling. Sprinkle top with confectioners' sugar. ✎

Cape Cod Chocolate Brownies

YIELD: 16 BROWNIES

Brownies:

1/2 cup butter

1 (4-ounce) bar sweet cooking
   chocolate

1/2 cup sugar

1 teaspoon vanilla extract

2 eggs

1 cup flour

1/2 teaspoon baking powder

1/4 teaspoon salt

Topping:

2 tablespoons butter, melted

1/2 cup firmly packed brown sugar

2 tablespoons corn syrup

2 tablespoons milk

1 cup coconut

1/2 cup finely chopped pecans

Preheat oven to 350°F. In medium saucepan, prepare brownies by melting butter with chocolate over low heat, stirring constantly. Cool slightly. Add sugar and vanilla, blending well. Add eggs and beat well. Add flour, baking powder, and salt and mix well. Spread in oiled 8 or 9-inch square pan.

Bake for 18 to 26 minutes, or until toothpick inserted in center comes out clean. Remove brownies from oven. Turn oven to broil.

Meanwhile, prepare topping. In small bowl, combine butter, brown sugar, corn syrup, and milk and blend well. Stir in coconut and pecans. Drop mixture by spoonfuls evenly over warm brownies; spread gently. Broil 4 inches from heat for 1 to 1 1/2 minutes or until bubbly. Cool completely and cut into bars. ❧

Cape Cod's Own Pecan Cake

YIELD: 9–12 SERVINGS

3/4 cup chopped pecans

6 peaches, peeled and sliced

1 (8-ounce) package cream cheese, softened

1 cup firmly packed light brown sugar

4 large eggs

1/2 cup half-and-half

1 1/2 teaspoons vanilla extract

1 cup (6-ounce package) almond brickle chips

1/2 cup coconut flakes

1/2 cup gingersnap cookie crumbs

Whipped cream (optional)

Preheat oven to 350°F and lightly grease a 9-inch square baking pan; set aside. Spread the pecans in single layer on ungreased baking sheet. Bake pecans until lightly browned—about 10 minutes—stirring occasionally. Chop peaches; set aside.

Beat softened cream cheese and brown sugar in large bowl until mixture is well blended. Add eggs, one at a time, beating well after each addition. Blend in half-and-half and vanilla extract. Stir in gingersnap cookie crumbs, brickle chips, toasted pecans, and coconut flakes. Next, stir in the chopped peaches and spread the mixture in the prepared baking pan.

Bake cake until center is firm and eggs are golden, about 35 to 40 minutes. Serve with whipped cream if desired. ∾

Carrot Pudding

YIELD: 8 SERVINGS

10 medium carrots

2 large eggs

1¹/₂ cups milk

1 cup shredded cheddar cheese

1 cup butter cracker crumbs

¹/₂ cup butter

¹/₂ teaspoon salt

¹/₄ teaspoon cayenne pepper

4 slices bacon

Peel carrots and cut into small slices.

Combine carrots with enough water to cover in a medium saucepan. Bring to a boil; reduce heat. Simmer carrots until tender (about 25 minutes) and drain well. Mash the carrots (should yield about 2 cups).

Preheat the oven to 350°F. Butter the bottom and sides of a 2-quart baking casserole.

Whisk eggs in a bowl until blended. Add carrots, milk, cheese, cracker crumbs, butter, salt, and cayenne pepper to eggs and mix well. Fry bacon until crisp and set aside. Spoon the carrot mixture into the prepared casserole. Bake for 30 minutes until set and lightly browned. Crumble the bacon and use to top the pudding. ∽

Chocolate Nut Angel Pie

YIELD: 6 TO 8 SERVINGS

Meringue:

1/2 cup sugar

1/8 teaspoon cream of tartar

2 egg whites

1/2 cup chopped pecans

Chocolate Filling:

3/4 cup semisweet chocolate bits

3 tablespoons hot water

1 teaspoon vanilla extract

1 cup heavy cream

Preheat oven to 275°F. To prepare meringue, sift together sugar and cream of tartar. Beat egg whites until stiff but not dry. Add sifted sugar gradually to the egg whites, beating well after each addition. Continue beating until the meringue is quite stiff and no sugar crystals are present. Fold in pecans. Butter a 9-inch pie plate and fill with the meringue. Do not bring out to the edge of the plate. Bake for about 1 hour or until delicately browned. Cool thoroughly.

To prepare chocolate filling, melt the chocolate in the top of a double boiler. Add the hot water and cook until thickened. Cool slightly. The mixture will become quite thick. Add the vanilla. Then whip the heavy cream and fold into the chocolate. Combine well but do not beat. Pour into the meringue shell. Chill 2 to 3 hours or refrigerate overnight before serving. ❧

Menemsha by-the-sea, Martha's Vineyard

Chocolate Swirl Cake

YIELD: 1 CAKE

Cake:

12-ounce package semisweet
   chocolate morsels

3 tablespoons water

2½ cups flour

1 teaspoon baking powder

1 teaspoon salt

1½ cups sugar

1 cup butter, softened

1 teaspoon vanilla extract

4 eggs

1 cup milk

Glaze:

½ cup semisweet chocolate morsels,
   reserved from 12-ounce package

¼ cup water

1 to 1½ cups confectioners' sugar

Preheat oven to 350°F. To prepare cake, combine over hot (not boiling) water 1½ cups chocolate morsels and water. Stir until smooth. In a bowl, combine flour, baking powder, and salt. In a separate bowl, cream sugar, butter, and vanilla. Beat in eggs, 1 at a time. Add flour mixture alternately with milk. Mix well.

Pour ⅓ of batter into oiled and floured 10-inch tube pan (not fluted pan). Spread with half the morsel mixture. Repeat layers. Swirl batter. Bake for 60 to 70 minutes. Cool for 15 to 20 minutes before removing from pan. Cool.

Meanwhile, while cake is baking, prepare the glaze. Combine over hot (not boiling) water chocolate morsels and water. Stir until smooth. Stir in confectioners' sugar until thoroughly combined.

Spoon glaze over cake. Let cake stand 15 minutes more before serving. ❧

Citrus Baked Alaska

YIELD: 4 SERVINGS

8 egg whites

1 cup superfine sugar

1/2 teaspoon vanilla extract

2 large grapefruits

8 scoops ice cream (1/2 cup each)

Preheat oven to 475°F. Beat egg whites to soft peak stage. Gradually add small amounts of sugar until dissolved in meringue. Beat until peaks stand up straight and glossy. Stabilize grapefruit halves by cutting a small slice off the bottom. Line up grapefruit halves on cookie sheet. Top with hardened scoops of ice cream. Carefully spread thick coating of meringue over ice cream and grapefruit cups. Brown in preheated oven for about 3 to 5 minutes, or until tips of meringue are golden. Serve immediately. ∿

Corn Pudding

YIELD: 6 TO 8 SERVINGS

2 packages frozen corn niblets

3 eggs

1/4 cup flour

1 tablespoon sugar

1/2 teaspoon salt

1/2 teaspoon white pepper

2 tablespoons melted butter

2 cups light cream

Cook corn according to package directions, reducing cooking time to just a few minutes. Drain and cool. Grind corn slightly in blender or food processor, working 1/3 of the mixture at a time.

Preheat oven to 325°F. In a separate bowl, beat the eggs well and then add the ground corn. Mix dry ingredients and add to corn mixture. Stir in butter and cream and mix thoroughly. Pour into well-oiled 1½-quart baking dish. Place baking dish in a larger pan of hot water. Bake for about 1 hour, or until firm and brown on top.

Cranberry Bread Pudding

YIELD: 10 SERVINGS

6 cups toasted whole wheat
  bread cubes

1 cup fresh or frozen cranberries

2 cups raspberry-cranberry drink

1 cup honey

1/2 cup butter

1 teaspoon cinnamon

1/2 teaspoon nutmeg

1 cup raisins

Grease a 2-quart casserole dish. Pour bread cubes into prepared casserole. Set aside. Combine all remaining ingredients in a large saucepan. Bring to a boil over medium heat. Boil gently just until the cranberries begin to pop. Pour cranberry mixture over bread cubes. Let sit 15 minutes.

Meanwhile, preheat oven to 350°F. Bake pudding for 45 minutes. Serve warm with vanilla ice cream. ❧

Cranberry Orange Pound Cake

YIELD: 16 SERVINGS

Cake:

2¾ cups sugar

1½ cups butter

1 teaspoon vanilla extract

1 teaspoon grated orange peel

6 eggs

3 cups flour

1 teaspoon baking powder

½ teaspoon salt

8 ounces (1 cup) dairy sour cream

1½ cups chopped fresh or frozen
   cranberries (do not thaw)

Butter Rum Sauce:

1 cup sugar

1 tablespoon flour

½ cup half-and-half

½ cup butter

4 teaspoons light rum

Preheat oven to 350°F. Generously grease and lightly flour 12-cup bundt pan. In large bowl, prepare cake by combining sugar and butter; beat until light and fluffy. Add vanilla and orange peel. Add eggs 1 at a time, beating well after each addition.

In medium bowl, combine flour, baking powder, and salt. Add alternately with sour cream, beating well after each addition. Gently stir in cranberries. Pour batter into greased and floured pan.

Bake for 65 to 75 minutes, or until toothpick inserted into center comes out clean. Cool 15 minutes. Remove from pan.

Meanwhile, prepare the sauce. In small saucepan, combine sugar and flour. Stir in half-and-half and butter. Cook over medium heat until thickened and bubbly, stirring constantly. Remove from heat; stir in rum. Serve warm sauce over cake.

Devil's Food Cake

YIELD: 8 SERVINGS

Cake:

2 cups flour

1 teaspoon baking soda

1 teaspoon salt

$1/2$ cup butter, softened

$1^1/2$ cups sugar

1 teaspoon vanilla extract

3 eggs, separated

2 ounces baker's chocolate, melted

1 cup buttermilk

Fudge Frosting:

3 tablespoons butter

$3/4$ cup sugar

$1/2$ cup unsweetened cocoa

3 tablespoons milk

1 teaspoon vanilla

Preheat oven to 400°F. Sift together flour, soda, and salt. Cream butter and sugar until fluffy; beat in vanilla and egg yolks. Mix well. Beat in melted chocolate. Add flour alternately with buttermilk, beating until smooth. Fold in stiffly beaten egg whites. Bake in an 8- or 9-inch square pan for 1 hour, or until done. Remove from pan and cool on a wire rack before serving.

While cake is baking, prepare frosting. Melt butter and sugar together in a saucepan over low to medium heat, stirring constantly. Add cocoa, milk, and vanilla, stir constantly, and simmer for 1 minute. Remove from heat and allow to cool slightly before spreading over top and sides of cake. ❧

English Apple and Prune Cake

YIELD: 8 OR 12 SERVINGS

1 stick of butter (4 ounces)

3/4 cup plus 3 tablespoons sugar

2 eggs, well beaten

1/2 cup self-rising flour

1/2 teaspoon baking powder

1/2 cup ground almonds

1/2 cup milk

1 teaspoon vanilla extract

1 tablespoon boiling water

8 pitted prunes, chopped

1/2 cup finely chopped walnuts, mixed with 3 tablespoons sugar

2 Granny Smith apples, cored and sliced, with peel left on

1 teaspoon cinnamon

Butter

Preheat oven to 375°F. Cream together butter, 3/4 cup sugar, and eggs until smooth. Add dry ingredients and ground almonds, along with milk, vanilla, and boiling water. Mix with electric mixer until smooth and well mixed.

Pour into a well-buttered 10-inch cake pan with removable bottom. Place the prunes on the batter, evenly spread over the top. Spoon the walnut and sugar mixture over the prunes. Then arrange the apple slices over the top of the walnuts.

Bake for 45 minutes. Remove from oven; sprinkle the top with cinnamon and 3 tablespoons sugar, dot with butter, and return to oven. Bake for 20 to 25 minutes more, or until a skewer comes out clean. Cool in the pan before serving.

Feather Cake

1/2 cup sifted flour

1/4 teaspoon mace

1/4 teaspoon cloves

7 eggs, separated

1 cup granulated sugar

2 teaspoons lemon juice

Peel of 1 lemon, finely grated

3/4 teaspoon cream of tartar

1/2 teaspoon salt

Preheat oven to 325°F. Line bottom of 10-inch tube pan with waxed paper. Sift together flour, mace, and cloves. Beat egg yolks until thick; add sugar gradually, and beat thoroughly, about 10 to 15 minutes. Beat in lemon juice and peel. Clean beaters. Beat whites until frothy and add cream of tartar and salt. Continue beating until firm peaks form. Heap mixture on top of egg yolks; add whites. Fold together only until blended. Pour into prepared pan. Bake for 45 minutes, or until cake tests done. Invert pan. Cool at least 1 hour. Serve frosted or unfrosted. ∿

Depot, Woods Hole

Flaming Cranberry Jubilee

YIELD: 8 SERVINGS

2 cups fresh or frozen whole
  cranberries

1 (8-ounce) jar plum jam

1/2 teaspoon cinnamon

1 quart vanilla ice cream

Sugar cubes

1/2 cup brandy or cognac

Simmer cranberries gently with jam and cinnamon for about 5 minutes on stovetop or in microwave. Cool. (Will keep for weeks in refrigerator, in tightly covered container.)

Scoop ice cream into serving dishes. Ladle on cranberry sauce and top with a sugar cube soaked in brandy or cognac. Light cube with a match and serve immediately. Flame will continue for several minutes. (Use caution.) ∾

Flourless Carrot Cake

YIELD: 1 CAKE

2 cups finely grated carrots

12 large eggs, separated

2 cups sugar

3/4 cup ground almonds

1/2 teaspoon ground cinnamon

1/2 teaspoon nutmeg

Preheat oven to 275°F. Remove as much liquid as possible from the carrots by squeezing them in a cheesecloth.

Beat the egg yolks with sugar until creamy. Add the carrots, almonds, and spices. In a separate bowl, beat the egg whites until they form tall, glistening peaks. The egg whites are done when you can cut through them and the mixture no longer runs. Do not overbeat. Gently fold the egg whites into the carrot mixture, making sure not to overmix. Gently pour the mixture into an oiled oblong (preferably Pyrex) 9 × 13-inch baking dish. Bake for about 1½ hours. ∾

Ginger Baked Apples with Warm Caramel Sauce

YIELD: 4 SERVINGS

Baked Apples:

4 cinnamon sticks

4 large, firm apples, cored

8 to 12 whole cloves

10 ounces ginger ale

1/2 lemon

Dash vanilla extract

Warm Caramel Sauce:

4 ounces (1 stick) unsalted butter

1 cup light brown sugar

1/2 teaspoon vanilla extract

1 cup heavy whipping cream

Preheat oven to 325°F. Place a cinnamon stick in the core of each apple. Insert 2 or 3 cloves into each apple, decoratively. Place apples in a deep baking dish with cover. Pour ginger ale over the apples. Place the half lemon in the center of the dish, in the middle of the apples. Sprinkle a dash of vanilla over the apples and cover the dish. Bake for 45 minutes, or until apples are soft but not mushy.

While apples are baking, prepare sauce. Melt butter and sugar in a saucepan over low heat, stirring to prevent burning. Add vanilla. Add cream, stirring constantly, and bring just to the point of simmer over low to medium heat. Reduce heat to prevent boiling. Continue to simmer for about 10 minutes, until thickened. Cool to warm before serving over baked apples. ～

Gingered Pear, Cranberry, and Blueberry Cobbler

YIELD: 6 TO 8 SERVINGS

Topping:

1 cup flour

1 teaspoon baking powder

1/4 cup sugar

3 tablespoons butter

2 egg whites, lightly beaten

1/4 cup skim milk

Fruit Mixture:

4 cups sliced, peeled fresh pears

2 cups fresh or frozen blueberries

1 cup fresh or frozen cranberries

1/2 cup sugar

2 tablespoons cornstarch

1 teaspoon ginger

Preheat oven to 400°F. In medium bowl, prepare topping by combining flour, baking powder, and sugar. Mix well. With pastry blender or fork, cut in butter until mixture is crumbly. Add egg whites and milk, stirring until well blended. Set aside.

In large bowl, combine all fruit mixture ingredients and mix well. Spray 8-inch square (2-quart) baking dish with nonstick cooking spray and spoon fruit mixture into baking dish. Spoon topping evenly over fruit mixture. Bake for 45 to 50 minutes, or until topping is golden brown. Serve warm with vanilla ice cream. ❧

Ball game, Evans Field, Provincetown

Great-Aunt Clara's Applesauce Cake

YIELD: 12 SERVINGS

Cake:

2 cups flour

1½ teaspoons baking soda

1½ teaspoons salt

2 tablespoons cocoa

½ teaspoon cinnamon

½ teaspoon cloves

½ teaspoon nutmeg

½ teaspoon allspice

1½ cups sugar

½ cup vegetable shortening

1½ cups applesauce

2 eggs, unbeaten

1 cup mixed diced candied fruit

½ cup chopped nuts

Cranberry Cream Frosting:

2 tablespoons vegetable shortening

1 tablespoon butter

1 teaspoon vanilla extract

¼ teaspoon salt

2½ cups confectioners' sugar

• • •

Sift flour, soda, salt, cocoa, spices, and sugar together. Add shortening and applesauce and beat for 2 minutes. Add 2 eggs and beat for 2 minutes more. Fold in fruit and nuts, mixing thoroughly. Bake in a greased, floured 10-inch tube pan. Bake at 325°F for 1 hour and 25 to 35 minutes.

While cake is baking, prepare frosting. Beat together all ingredients. When cake cools, frost with Cranberry Cream frosting.

Lemon Chiffon Cheesecake with Fruit Topping

YIELD: 16 SERVINGS

Crust:

1³/4 cups gingersnap crumbs
  (about 30 cookies)

¹/4 cup butter, melted

Filling:

3 (8-ounce) packages cream
  cheese

1 cup sugar

4 eggs

1 (15- or 16-ounce) can lemon
  pie filling

1 (8-ounce) container sour cream

1 teaspoon grated lemon peel

Preheat oven to 350°F. In medium bowl, combine crust ingredients and mix well. Press into bottom and ¹/2 inch up sides of 9-inch springform pan. Bake for 5 minutes.

Meanwhile, prepare filling. In large bowl, combine cream cheese and sugar and beat at low speed until light and fluffy. Add eggs, 1 at a time, beating well after each addition. Reserve ¹/2 cup pie filling for topping. Add remaining pie filling, sour cream, and grated lemon peel and blend well. Pour filling over crust into pan, spreading evenly. Bake at 350°F for 70 to 80 minutes. (To minimize cracking, place shallow pan half full of hot water on lower oven rack during baking.) Cool on wire rack for 1 hour. Cover and refrigerate at least 24 hours.

(continued)

. . . continued

Topping:

3/4 cup raspberry jelly

2 teaspoons lemon juice

2 tablespoons orange liqueur

2 cups halved strawberries

1 cup blueberries

1 cup raspberries

2 kiwi fruit, peeled, quartered
   lengthwise, and sliced

Strips of lemon peel

To prepare topping, combine jelly and lemon juice in small microwave-safe bowl. Microwave on High for 30 to 60 seconds, stirring once. With wire whisk, stir until smooth. Add 2 tablespoons orange liqueur and blend well.

When ready to serve, remove sides of pan; place cheesecake on serving plate. Spread reserved pie filling over top of cheesecake. In medium bowl, combine strawberries, blueberries, and raspberries. Spoon about 1 cup berry mixture around edge of cheesecake. Drizzle with some of jelly mixture. Arrange a few kiwi pieces in berry mixture on cheesecake. Garnish with lemon peel strips. Serve with remaining fruit and jelly mixture. Store in refrigerator. ∾

Lemon Cream Pie

YIELD: 8 OR 10 SERVINGS

Pastry Pie Shell:

1/2 cup unsalted butter

1 1/2 cups flour

1 egg

3 tablespoons milk

Preheat oven to 425°F. To prepare pie crust, cut butter into flour until mixture is crumbly in medium mixing bowl. In small bowl, beat egg and milk together with a fork. Add to flour mixture, stirring with fork until mixture leaves sides of bowl and forms a ball. On lightly floured surface, knead dough 10 times. Divide dough into 2 balls and flatten; wrap tightly in plastic wrap. Refrigerate 30 to 60 minutes.

On lightly floured surface, roll out 1 ball of dough into an 11-inch circle. Place in a 9-inch pie pan and trim and crimp edge. Bake for 10 minutes. (Reserve remaining dough for another pie shell.)

(continued)

... continued

Filling:

1 cup sugar

$1/4$ cup cornstarch

$1/8$ teaspoon salt

$1^1/2$ cups milk

3 egg yolks, slightly beaten

$1/4$ cup unsalted butter

$1/4$ cup lemon juice

2 teaspoons grated lemon peel

$1/2$ cup dairy sour cream

1 cup whipping cream,
    sweetened, whipped

In a 2-quart saucepan, combine sugar, cornstarch, salt, and milk to prepare filling. Cook over medium heat, stirring constantly, until mixture comes to a full boil (10 to 12 minutes). Reduce heat to low, stirring constantly, for 2 minutes. Remove from heat. In small bowl, gradually stir 1 cup of hot milk mixture into egg yolks. Return mixture to saucepan. Cook over medium heat, stirring constantly for 2 minutes. Remove from heat. Stir in butter, lemon juice, and lemon peel until butter is melted. Stir in sour cream. Pour into pie shell. Refrigerate until firm (2 to 3 hours). Garnish with whipped cream.

Maple Walnut Tart

1/2 cup pure maple syrup

1/2 cup water

3 tablespoons cornstarch

4 tablespoons butter

Pie pastry for a single crust pie (use your favorite recipe or already-made dough)

1 cup shelled walnuts

Bring maple syrup and water to a boil and cook for 5 minutes. Mix water and cornstarch together and then add cornstarch mixture to maple syrup. Add butter and stir until butter is melted and incorporated. Let mixture cool to lukewarm.

Preheat oven to 425°F. Line an 8- to 10-inch tart pan with the pastry dough. Spread syrup mixture over pastry crust and then scatter walnuts over top. Bake for 20 minutes. Serve warm or cold. May be served with whipped cream or vanilla ice cream. ◕

Old-Fashioned Apple Blueberry Cake

YIELD: 8 TO 10 SERVINGS

$1/2$ cup unsalted butter

$1/4$ cup whipping cream

$1^1/4$ cups sugar

3 eggs

$2^1/3$ cups flour

2 teaspoons baking powder

1 teaspoon salt

2 cups tart cooking apples (about 2 medium), peeled, cored, and coarsely chopped

2 cups blueberries

Heavy cream, for whipping

Preheat oven to 350°F. In a 1-quart saucepan, melt butter into cream over low heat, stirring often. Remove from heat when butter is melted and set aside. In large mixing bowl, combine sugar and eggs. Beat at medium speed, scraping sides of bowl often, until well mixed (1 to 2 minutes). Add butter mixture, flour, baking powder, and salt. Continue beating, scraping sides of bowl often, until smooth (1 to 2 minutes). Stir in apples and blueberries.

Spread into oiled and floured 13 × 9-inch baking pan. Bake for 45 minutes or until wooden pick inserted in center comes out clean. Serve warm with unsweetened whipped cream. ❧

Orange Crème Brûlée

YIELD: 8 SERVINGS

2 cups whipping cream

3/4 cup orange liqueur

3 eggs

3 egg yolks

1/4 cup white sugar

1/4 cup firmly packed brown
   sugar

Preheat oven to 325°F. Place 1½-quart casserole in a 9 × 13-inch pan. In medium saucepan, heat whipping cream and liqueur over medium-low heat just until hot. Do not boil. Set aside.

(continued)

. . . continued

In medium bowl, combine eggs, egg yolks, and white sugar. Stir with spoon until well blended. Gradually add hot cream mixture to egg mixture, stirring constantly. Strain mixture through fine strainer into casserole. Set pan with casserole into oven. Pour hot water into pan halfway up sides of casserole.

Bake for 25 to 30 minutes, or until mixture is set when casserole is jiggled. Remove from oven. Cool 30 minutes. Cover with casserole lid or plastic wrap, not allowing plastic wrap to touch surface of custard. Refrigerate overnight or at least 8 hours.

When ready to serve, carefully blot any surface moisture from top of custard with paper towel. Spoon brown sugar into fine strainer. With fingers or back of spoon, press brown sugar through strainer evenly over top of custard.

Broil 6 to 8 inches from heat for 30 to 60 seconds, or until brown sugar is melted and bubbly, rotating or moving dish if sugar is melting unevenly. Watch carefully. (Topping burns easily.) Cool 2 minutes to harden sugar. Serve immediately. ∾

Peach Cobbler

YIELD: 6 TO 8 SERVINGS

1/2 cup butter, melted

4 to 5 tree-ripened peaches

1 1/2 cups sugar

1 cup flour

2 teaspoons baking powder

Pinch of cinnamon

Pinch of nutmeg

1/4 teaspoon salt

1 cup milk

Preheat oven to 350°F. Butter and flour a 9 × 13-inch glass baking dish. Pour melted butter into the dish. In a saucepan, slowly cook the peaches with 1/2 cup sugar until soft. In a bowl, combine flour with remaining sugar, baking powder, cinnamon, nutmeg, and salt. Whisk in milk and mix thoroughly. Pour batter into baking dish over butter. Gently pour cooked peaches evenly over batter. Bake for 45 minutes or until golden brown. ❧

Circuit Avenue looking south, Oak Bluffs

Peach Pudding

YIELD: 4 TO 6 SERVINGS

8 gingersnap cookies

1/2 teaspoon fresh ginger

4 fresh peaches, peeled and
  sliced

8 ounces cream cheese, softened

2 6-ounce containers of peach
  yogurt

1 teaspoon vanilla extract

Crush gingersnap cookies. Combine cookie crumbs and fresh ginger in small bowl and set aside. Coarsely chop peaches and set aside. Beat softened cream cheese in a small bowl with an electric mixer at medium speed until light and fluffy. Add peach yogurt and vanilla extract. Beat at low speed until mixture is smooth and well blended. Gently stir in chopped peaches.

Divide the peach mixture among four dessert bowls or parfait glasses. Cover tightly with plastic wrap and chill for 2 hours. Just before serving, top peach mixture with cookie crumb mixture. ◡

Pear Cranberry Apricot Cobbler

YIELD: 8 TO 10 SERVINGS

Topping:

1¼ cups flour

½ cup sugar

1 teaspoon baking powder

¼ teaspoon salt

¼ cup milk

1 tablespoon butter, melted

2 eggs

Fruit Mixture:

4 cups (4 to 5 medium) peeled, sliced pears

1 cup fresh or frozen whole cranberries

1 (16-ounce) can apricot halves, undrained

½ cup sugar

¾ teaspoon cinnamon

2 to 3 teaspoons grated orange peel

To prepare topping, combine flour, sugar, baking powder, and salt in medium bowl, blending well. Add milk, butter, and eggs, mixing until batter is smooth. Set aside.

Preheat oven to 350°F. In medium saucepan, combine all fruit mixture ingredients. Cook over medium heat, stirring occasionally, for 10 to 15 minutes, or until mixture is hot. Pour hot fruit mixture into greased 2-quart casserole; top with batter. Bake for 30 to 40 minutes, or until topping is golden brown. Serve warm. ✧

Pumpkin Cake

YIELD: 9 SERVINGS

Cake:

1/2 cup shortening

1 1/4 cups sugar

2 eggs

1 1/4 cups sifted cake flour

1 tablespoon baking powder

1/2 teaspoon salt

1/2 teaspoon ground cinnamon

1/2 teaspoon ground ginger

1/2 teaspoon ground nutmeg

1 cup cooked and cooled fresh pumpkin or canned pumpkin

1/4 cup milk

1/4 teaspoon baking soda

1/2 cup chopped nuts

Preheat oven to 350°F. Prepare the cake by creaming the shortening in a large mixing bowl. Gradually add the sugar, beating until light and fluffy. Beat in the eggs. In a medium bowl, sift together the cake flour, baking powder, salt, cinnamon, ginger, and nutmeg. Combine the pumpkin and milk. Stir in the baking soda. Add the flour and pumpkin mixtures alternately to the shortening-sugar mixture, beating well after each addition. Fold in nuts.

Turn the batter into a greased 9 × 9 × 2-inch baking pan lined with waxed paper. Bake for 50 minutes. Cool in the pan on a wire rack for 10 minutes. Turn the cake out onto the rack; remove the waxed paper and cool completely.

(continued)

... continued

Raisin-Brown Sugar Icing:

1 large egg white

1 cup packed light brown sugar

3 tablespoons water

$^{1}/_{2}$ cup coarsely chopped raisins

Prepare the frosting while the cake is baking. In the top of a double boiler, beat together the egg white, brown sugar, and water until just blended. Place the mixture over rapidly boiling water and beat with a rotary beater or an electric mixer for 5 to 7 minutes, or until the mixture is light and fluffy and holds stiff peaks. Remove from heat. Carefully fold in the raisins. When cake is cooled completely, frost the top and sides with the icing. ∾

Raspberry Breakfast Cake

Cake:

3/4 cup sugar

1/2 cup butter, softened

3 eggs

1/3 cup mashed ripe bananas
  (1 small banana)

1/4 cup milk

1/4 cup dairy sour cream

1 teaspoon almond extract

2 cups flour

1 1/2 teaspoons baking powder

1 1/2 cups fresh or frozen raspberries, thawed and drained

Frosting:

1 cup powdered sugar

1/4 cup butter, softened

1 to 2 teaspoons lemon juice

Preheat oven to 350°F. In large bowl, prepare cake by combining sugar, butter, eggs, and banana; beat until light and fluffy. Beat in milk, sour cream, and almond extract. Add flour and baking powder to banana mixture, stirring just until dry ingredients are moistened. Pour half of batter into greased and floured 9-inch square pan. Spread raspberries over batter and then cover with remaining batter. Bake for 50 to 55 minutes, or until top is a deep golden brown. Cool 45 to 60 minutes.

To prepare frosting, in small bowl, beat powdered sugar and butter until well blended. Add enough lemon juice to make desired spreading consistency. Spread on warm cake. Cut into squares to serve. Serve warm. ⌒

Rhubarb Cake

YIELD: 12 SERVINGS

Topping:

1/2 cup sugar

1 tablespoon cinnamon

Cake:

1/2 cup butter

1 1/2 cups sugar

1 egg

2 1/2 cups flour

1/2 teaspoon salt

1 cup milk

1 teaspoon vanilla extract

2 cups chopped rhubarb

Preheat oven to 350°F. Prepare topping by mixing sugar and cinnamon together.

To prepare cake, cream butter and sugar and add egg and vanilla. Add dry ingredients alternately with milk. Add rhubarb and mix. Sprinkle topping over cake. Pour into 9 × 13-inch pan and bake for 35 to 45 minutes. ∽

Rum Cheesecake

Crust:

1 1/2 cups graham cracker crumbs

1/2 cup butter, melted

1/4 cup sugar

Filling:

12 ounces butterscotch morsels

16 ounces plain cream cheese, softened

1/4 cup sugar

1/4 teaspoon salt

3 eggs

3 cups sour cream

1/2 cup dark rum

1/4 cup milk

Preheat oven to 375°F. Combine all crust ingredients and mix well. Press onto bottom and 1 3/4 inches up the sides of a 10-inch springform pan. Bake for 10 minutes. Remove from oven, set aside, and cool.

To prepare filling, melt morsels over hot (not boiling) water and stir until smooth. Remove from heat and let cool for 30 minutes. Beat together cream cheese, sugar, salt, and melted morsels until smooth. Add eggs and beat in mixer on low speed just until combined. Do not overbeat. Add sour cream, rum, and milk, stirring just until combined. Pour into crust.

Bake for 45 minutes. Remove from oven and let stand for 15 minutes. Loosen sides of cake from pan and cool for 30 minutes more. Remove sides of pan. Refrigerate for 6 to 8 hours before serving. ∾

Old mill, Nantucket

Rum Raisin Rice Pudding

YIELD: 6 SERVINGS

$1/2$ cup golden raisins

$1/4$ cup dark rum

$2^1/2$ cups milk

1 cup long grain rice

$1/2$ cup firmly packed light
brown sugar

$1/2$ cup sugar

2 tablespoons unsalted butter

1 teaspoon salt

$1/4$ teaspoon ground cinnamon

$1^1/2$ cups half-and-half

1 tablespoon cornstarch

3 large egg yolks, lightly beaten

$1^1/2$ teaspoons vanilla extract

In a small saucepan, combine the raisins and rum. Bring to a boil over medium-high heat. Remove from heat and let steep while making the pudding.

In a medium saucepan, combine the milk, rice, brown sugar, sugar, butter, salt, cinnamon, and 1 cup of half-and-half. Cook over medium heat until milk mixture comes to a gentle boil. Stir the mixture, cover the pan, and reduce heat to low. Cook 40 to 45 minutes, or until the rice is cooked through and much of the liquid is absorbed.

(continued)

. . . continued

Place the cornstarch in a small bowl. Gradually whisk in the remaining 1/2 cup half-and-half until smooth. Whisk in the egg yolks. Whisk about 1/2 cup of the hot rice mixture into the egg mixture. Return this mixture to the pudding in the saucepan. Cook over medium heat until the mixture just starts to bubble. Continue to cook, stirring, for 1 minute, or until the mixture thickens slightly. Remove from heat.

Add the vanilla to the rum raisin mixture and stir the mixture into the rice pudding. Divide the pudding among 6 dessert dishes or parfait glasses and cover with plastic wrap (unless you want a skin to form), pressing the wrap directly onto the surface of the pudding. Refrigerate until well chilled, about 2 hours.

Sour Cream Apple Pie

YIELD: 8 SERVINGS

Crust for 9-inch pie

Filling:

6 large cooking apples

1 cup sour cream

1/3 cup sugar

1 egg, beaten

1/4 teaspoon salt

1 teaspoon vanilla extract

1/4 cup flour

Zest of 1 lemon

Topping:

1/4 cup brown sugar

1 teaspoon cinnamon

1/4 cup sugar

1 cup chopped walnuts

Preheat oven to 350°F. Place crust in pie plate. Peel, core, and slice apples. Mix sour cream, sugar, egg, salt, vanilla, flour, and zest in a bowl. Add sliced apples to mixture. Pour into pie shell. Mix together topping and spread over pie. Bake for 55 to 60 minutes.

Spiced Chocolate Cake

YIELD: 8 TO 10 SERVINGS

Cake:

3/4 cup butter

1 1/2 cups sugar

3 eggs, beaten

2 cups cake flour

1/2 teaspoon baking powder

1/2 teaspoon baking soda

1 teaspoon salt

3/4 teaspoon ground nutmeg

1 teaspoon cinnamon

1/2 cup milk

1 teaspoon lemon juice

1 teaspoon vanilla extract

1/2 cup walnut meats, toasted and coarsely chopped

Icing:

6 tablespoons butter

1 egg yolk

3 cups confectioners' sugar

1 tablespoon cocoa

1 teaspoon cinnamon

1 1/2 tablespoons powdered (instant) coffee

• • •

Preheat oven to 350°F. To prepare cake, cream butter and sugar until light and fluffy. Add eggs and mix well. Sift together dry ingredients. Mix milk, lemon juice, and vanilla. Add dry ingredients alternately with milk mixture to butter and egg mixture, beating well with each addition. When thoroughly blended, fold in nutmeats.

Divide batter between 2 oiled and floured 8-inch layer pans. Bake for 30 minutes. Cool on wire rack.

While cake is baking, prepare icing. Cream butter and egg yolk. Sift together sugar, cocoa, and cinnamon. Add to butter mixture. Blend well. Beat in coffee and mix well. Spread a thin layer of icing between cakes and ice top and sides. ❧

Strawberry Mousse

YIELD: 6 TO 8 SERVINGS

16 ounces frozen strawberries in syrup

2 cups heavy whipping cream

1/4 cup confectioners' sugar

1/2 teaspoon vanilla extract

Fresh whole strawberries, for garnish

Thaw frozen strawberries and strain to separate most of the syrup. Keep 1/2 cup syrup and discard the rest. Beat together the whipping cream and confectioners' sugar until it begins to thicken. Add the vanilla extract. Slowly beat the strawberry syrup into the cream. Continue to beat until stiff peaks are formed.

To serve, divide the thawed, sliced strawberries and place in the bottoms of 6 to 8 serving dishes or champagne flutes. Spoon the mousse over the top and garnish with fresh, whole berries on top.

Strawberry Summer Soup

YIELD: 8 SERVINGS

2 pints fresh strawberries

1 quart plain yogurt

1 quart orange juice

$^1/_2$ cup sugar

$^3/_4$ cup honey

Sliced strawberries, for garnish

Mint, for garnish

*W*ash and hull strawberries. Put into food processor and chop (not too fine). Mix with yogurt, orange juice, sugar, and honey. Chill. Ladle soup into bowls. Garnish with sliced strawberries and a sprig of fresh mint, and a dollop of yogurt. ❧

Whiskey Cake

YIELD: 8 TO 10 SERVINGS

1^1/$_2$ cups seedless raisins

2 cups water

^{3}/$_4$ cup sugar

^{1}/$_2$ cup butter

1 egg

1^1/$_2$ cups sifted flour

1 teaspoon baking soda

^{1}/$_2$ teaspoon nutmeg

^{1}/$_4$ teaspoon allspice

^{1}/$_2$ teaspoon salt

1 cup chopped walnuts

^{1}/$_2$ cup Bourbon whiskey

^{1}/$_2$ teaspoon ground cloves

Shelled walnut halves

Cover raisins with water and simmer, uncovered, for 20 minutes. Drain, saving ^{3}/$_4$ cup cooking liquid. Cool.

Preheat oven to 350°F. Cream sugar and butter together thoroughly. Beat in egg. Sift together flour, baking soda, nutmeg, allspice, and salt. Blend into creamed mixture alternately with cooking liquid. Stir in raisins, nuts, and whiskey. Pour into 2 oiled 9-inch layer pans. Bake for about 25 minutes. Remove from pans and cool thoroughly.

(continued)

. . . continued

Bourbon Hard Sauce:

¹/₄ cup butter, softened

3 cups sifted confectioners' sugar

1 small egg, beaten

3 tablespoons Bourbon whiskey

While cake is baking, cream butter and gradually beat in the sugar alternately with the egg and whiskey. If not thin enough to spread, add additional whiskey by the spoonful. Frost tops and sides of cakes with Bourbon Hard Sauce. Decorate top of cakes with walnut halves. ☙

White Chocolate Ladyfinger Cake

YIELD: 10 TO 12 SERVINGS

Cake:

12 ounces white chocolate
   baking bars

$1^{1}/_{2}$ cups heavy whipping cream

8 ounces cream cheese, softened

6-ounce package of ladyfinger
   cookies

$^{1}/_{4}$ cup espresso or French Roast
   brewed coffee

1 tablespoon rum, or
   $^{1}/_{2}$ teaspoon rum extract

*I*n top of double boiler over hot (not boiling) water, melt white chocolate bars with $^{1}/_{4}$ cup cream. Stir until melted and smooth. In large mixing bowl, beat cream cheese until blended and fluffy. Gradually add melted chocolate, beating well after each addition. In small mixing bowl, beat remaining cream until stiff peaks form. Fold into cream cheese chocolate mixture and set aside.

Line bottom and sides of 9 × 3-inch springform pan with wax paper. Line bottom and sides with ladyfinger halves, split sides up. In small bowl, combine coffee and rum. Brush about half of coffee mixture onto ladyfingers in pan. Spoon half of cream cheese chocolate mixture over ladyfingers in pan. Repeat ladyfinger, coffee, and cheese layers.

(continued)

. . . continued

Nutmeg Whipped Cream:

$1/2$ cup heavy whipping cream

2 tablespoons confectioners' sugar

$1/4$ teaspoon vanilla extract

$1/8$ teaspoon ground nutmeg

In small mixer bowl, prepare cream by beating heavy whipping cream, confectioners' sugar, vanilla extract, and ground nutmeg until stiff peaks form. Top the cake with the cream, and cover and refrigerate for at least 2 hours before serving. Remove side of pan. Garnish with fresh fruit before serving, if desired. ∾

Zabaglione

6 egg yolks

1/4 cup sugar

Dash of salt

1/3 cup Marsala

In top part of double boiler, with electric hand mixer set at medium speed, beat egg yolks, sugar, and salt until light and fluffy, about 1 minute. Gradually add Marsala, beating to combine well. Over hot (not boiling) water, beat at medium speed for 4 minutes, or until mixture begins to hold its shape. Do not overcook. Serve warm in sherbet glasses or as a sauce over poached fruit.

Sorting cranberries, Cape Cod

Beverages

Awesome Alligator

8 ounces cranberry-strawberry drink

3/4 ounce cream of coconut

Dash of Grenadine syrup

Club soda (optional)

Whipped cream, for garnish

Cherry or strawberry, for garnish

Put all ingredients, except soda and garnishes, in a blender. Blend for a few seconds on high speed, or until ingredients are thoroughly combined. Pour into a tall glass with crushed ice. Top with club soda, if desired. Garnish with whipped cream and a cherry or strawberry. ❧

Frozen Cranberry Margarita

5 ounces whole berry cranberry
   sauce

1¹/₂ ounces white tequila

¹/₂ ounce triple sec

1¹/₂ ounces lime juice

5 ounces crushed ice

Strawberry fan, for garnish

Put all ingredients, except garnish, in a blender. Blend for a few seconds on high speed, or until ingredients are thoroughly combined. Pour into large glass. Garnish with strawberry fan. ᴄ

Ginger Ale Lemonade

YIELD: 1 SERVING

3 lemons

1 cup sugar

1½ pints water

1 pint of ginger ale

Place a large piece of ice in a glass pitcher. Add the juice of the lemons, sugar, and water and thoroughly mix. Stir until sugar is dissolved. Add the ginger ale and serve immediately. ∾

Raspberry Kiss

YIELD: 1 SERVING

6 ounces cranberry-raspberry drink

1 ounce orange juice

¼ teaspoon lime juice

Club soda

Pour cranberry-raspberry drink, orange juice, and lime juice into a tall glass filled with ice. Top with club soda. ∾

Sunrise over Provincetown

1 (10-ounce) package frozen strawberries in syrup, thawed and drained

3 cups tangerine juice (made from frozen concentrate)

2 (750-ml) bottles champagne

6 fresh strawberries, with stems, halved, for garnish

Orange peel strips, for garnish

In blender container, puree frozen strawberries. In nonmetallic bowl, combine strawberry puree, tangerine juice, and champagne, mixing gently. Serve over ice in goblets. Garnish each glass with strawberry half and orange peel strips. ❧

White Sangria

1 cup sugar

1 cup water

1 cinnamon stick

2 medium oranges, sliced

1 lemon, sliced

1 lime, sliced

3 (750-ml) bottles dry, white wine, chilled

3 cups club soda, chilled

In medium saucepan, combine sugar, water, and cinnamon stick. Simmer 5 minutes over low heat. Remove from heat and add fruit. Cool completely, about 20 minutes. Remove cinnamon stick. Add white wine and mix gently but thoroughly. Add chilled club soda and mix gently immediately before serving. Serve from large pitcher or punch bowl. ∾

Index